THE NEXT WITNESS

Prophet-Editors
of
The Book of
Mormon

NATHAN E. LAMBERT

Print ISBN: 978-1-66785-455-7
eBook ISBN: 978-1-66785-456-4

Sterling & Judy,

whose encouragement and friendship

inspired this work.

ACKNOWLEDGEMENTS

First and foremost I would like to thank my dear Amy, as we are several roses into our forever together. Her patience with me has made this book possible.

Lee Green, for the tune-up on the first draft, and whose example through the years inspired me to seek his advice in this area. One never knows who is watching.

Sue Nelson, Shari Hurst, and Natalie Lambert.

May this work be a blessing to all who read it... and may you have friends like these.

PREFACE

I grew up in this city, and for as long as I can remember there was a line through the maps, a course through the suburbs, marked as the right of way for the West Valley Freeway. I moved into our home in the south-valley area and my commute to work was surface streets. There were two different general ways to get there, but they were both about the same: About 25 minutes.

Then the new freeway was finally built. It was a road without addresses, but it became an integral part of the traffic grid. My commute became 12 minutes. Like most of us, over time I adapted the directions to almost all destinations in the south valley to include this highway. Getting there has become easier. Those that have moved in since never knew the privation.

Like the local freeway, whose right of way had cut an unused line through the orchards and suburbs for as long as I can remember, you may have already seen or experienced the footprint of this concept: Like the local freeway, it would appear that when one realizes the pattern and purpose of the three primary editors of *The Book of Mormon*, that this concept can become the artery through which most other lessons of the book can be mapped, and even more certainly the tool to enhance perception of instruction that might have been previously hidden to us.

CHAPTER 1

In the Rough

For some, this might uncover additional insight into a book of scripture, the study of which has been a life-long passion, while for others, this will be the first glimpse of what can become a beautiful friendship. In either case and for anyone in between, I ask your permission to take you on what will at first seem to be an outing into the tall grass but assure you that it is a tour of the fairway. In other words, once you see it, you will not un-see it.

This message will enhance your understanding of some of the basic tenants that you may already hold close: Joseph Smith is the prophet through whom the gospel of Jesus Christ was restored in this dispensation. The Restoration is ongoing through living prophets today. *The Book of Mormon* is true, plays a role in the restoration of the gospel, and strengthens our ability to receive and to understand the will of God.

Mormon, his son Moroni, and Nephi(1) were not only the primary abridgers of the record we know as *The Book of Mormon*, but that they were also *editors:* They each specifically compiled this record from the originally written history to produce a manual to teach a seer—who would translate this work—to be a prophet of God.

Most of us read *The Book of Mormon* as a chronicle of events, sifting its annals for the precious gems of doctrine and of example. In so doing, we often bump up against or skip over certain anomalies that don't fit our idea of proper history. For example, Nephi including two visions of Lehi in the first 15 verses of his small plates, which were hearsay via Nephi and most certainly already contained in the lost 116 pages of manuscript referred to as the book of Lehi. We will recognize that items from the original historical record were hand-picked for use in the text and that those and many of the other "anomalies" are not inconsistencies at all, but that they verify that it is primarily a precisely-edited manual that is secondarily a history.

We will cover a lot of ground to demonstrate this. Here are a few of the highlights:

The purpose of the inclusion of the Isaiah chapters will be manifest. As I have come to understand why Nephi appreciated them, they have become some of my favorite studies.

We will discuss Brigham Young's testimony in the presence of Joseph Smith that modern revelation was even more important than the scriptures that the saints had received. In other words, as important as *The Book of Mormon* and *The Bible* are, modern revelation surpasses them both. As an example: were this not the case, Mormon might have followed the precedent of Ether by hiding and protecting the records instead of rejoining and leading the doomed Nephite army.

We note biblical precedence for the preparation of Joseph Smith by the prophet-editors of *The Book of Mormon*: That the prophet Samuel called Saul to "prophesy among the prophets."

gifts of prophesy and revelation. Not just the leaders but also those who are led. Having much more universal access can only bring greater peace among all earth dwellers.

I can state with certainty that when one heightens his awareness of *The Book of Mormon* as the revelation training manual that it was designed to be, *The Book of Mormon* will become an extremely useful tool for the saints to prepare themselves for the Millennium.

And once you see it....you will also see that *The Book of Mormon* deserves exploration via the prospective of its three prophet-editors.

CHAPTER 2

Editors of *The Book of Mormon*

Years ago my father-in-law worked as a research nuclear phys-
icist at a large company. This company had a local primary
campus known as "The Plant." In one of the buildings there was
a row of the offices of the seven local physicists, six of whom were
coincidently named "Bob". Each of the offices was the same size,
each had glass on the upper half of the wall facing the hallway, and
each of the first six doors had a simple sign designation with only
the name of the occupant: "Bob—" followed by his last name.
All had a modest placard except for the last door. Though perhaps
the most junior in age, she was not inferior in her education. In a
vocation that was at the time dominated by men, and tiring from
requests of others thinking that she was secretary to the other six
offices, she intentionally included a second placard with a complete
listing of her degrees.

We should begin our study by recognizing some titles pertaining specifically to the creation of *The Book of Mormon*. As we will
examine in this work, the bearers of these titles would humbly not
include them on their office doors, but there is some learning that
can come from understanding them.

Mormon abridged the majority of *The Book of Mormon*.

> *The Book of Mormon*, **Title Page**
>
> Wherefore, it is an abridgment of the record of the people of Nephi, and also of the Lamanites...

To abridge means to shorten by the omission of words without the sacrifice of sense. Mormon was an abridger. Moroni was an abridger:

> *The Book of Mormon*, **Title Page**
>
> An abridgment taken from the Book of Ether also...

And Nephi (1) was an abridger:

> **2 Nephi 9:2**
>
> 2 And now, as I have spoken concerning these plates, behold they are not the plates upon which I make a full account of the history of my people; for the plates upon which I make a full account of my people I have given the name of Nephi; wherefore, they are called the plates of Nephi, after mine own name; and these plates also are called the plates of Nephi.

We accept that *The Book of Mormon* was abridged by Mormon and Moroni, and also Nephi, but we do not often see them as editors also. Editing is a critical task in the abridging work as it determines the criteria of acceptance of various parts of the record into the final draft of the manuscript and fits the pieces together so that they are accurate, make sense, and teach the desired concepts to the target audiences. For example, Nephi stated in the very next verse:

> **1 Nephi 9:3**
>
> **3** Nevertheless, I have received a commandment of the Lord that I should make these plates, for the special purpose that there should be an account engraven of the ministry of my people.

More than just abridging, Nephi explicitly filtered the commonplace from the records and included specific teaching ("ministry") to a specific audience ("my people.") This is editing, not in the simplistic, proofreading sense, but in the global sense: Nephi reduces the text to serve a "special purpose." We will demonstrate how this is also the case with Mormon and Moroni.

Though editors usually play an invisible role in the production of a book, writer-editors such as these, play a prominent role not only because they lived in that era, but because the narrative, the history, the information, and the doctrine are all filtered through their lenses. The doctrine taught by Abinadi was remembered and written by Alma, and later edited by Mormon into what we have today. A simple abridgement might have excluded this important sermon completely, struck off because it occurred on a parallel time-line and not directly in the nation of the Nephite kings.

The role of an editor of scripture requires a particular set of skills and a special connection with deity. One of these is to be a seer:

> **Mosiah 8:15-16**
>
> **15** And the king said that a seer is greater than a prophet.
>
> **16** And Ammon said that a seer is a revelator and a prophet also; and a gift which is greater can no man have, except he should possess the power of God, which no man can; yet a man may have great power given him from God.

Not all prophets are seers, but all seers are prophets. While we may not know all of the special skills and requirements, we do know that these three editors, as well as he who would translate *The Book of Mormon* in this dispensation were called of God to be seers. (1 Nephi 10:7, Words of Mormon 1:9, Moroni 1:1-4, *Doctrine and Covenants* 21:1)

Recognizing that they held many other important and secular titles as leaders of their people—for this work we will list the following on each of the office doors of Mormon, Moroni, and Nephi: Prophet, Seer, Revelator, Writer, Abridger and Editor.

CHAPTER 3

White Water

In 1848, Gold was discovered in California at Sutter's Mill on the South Fork of the American River. Today, that section of the river is also a popular run for white-water rafting, with several Class III+ rapids. And there are at least 20 white-water rafting companies whose business is to make sure you have a thrilling and safe experience on this part of the river. The white-water enthusiasts have worked out a deal with the water-resources board so the out-flow from Chili Bar Dam above, though reduced most of the day, is increased for a few hours in the morning to create a nice ride for the rafts. The window of extra water-flow is listed in a published schedule throughout the rafting season.

Several years ago, I was training with several of my friends to be a river-rafting guide for that segment. The training involved a series of practice runs so we could become acquainted with that particular water. For each run, we would get up early on a Saturday morning, grab breakfast, drive three hours to the river, and get the equipment set up and the boats inflated. We would put in at a park designated for such a purpose, located on the downstream edge of the Marshall Gold-Discovery Park, and take out 12 miles later, at the bridge where the river becomes Folsom Reservoir. Then we would stow and return the equipment, with a stop halfway home for an early dinner, at a chain known for its really good burgers and really short fries.

The rapids, especially the Class III+ rapids, have names, like "Bouncing Rock," "Satan's Cesspool," and "Deadman's Drop." For each of these rapids there is a method that enables passage in a way that affords fun and perhaps keeps everyone on board. We learn to train our paddlers, determine the value of the power of our team, and how to use it along with our knowledge of the river to put the boat in the correct place, speed, and orientation. This is why we practice.

A good day on the river was when no one got hurt. (Those were all good days for us.) A great day on the river was when we hit "Hospital Bar" right on the mark. Hospital Bar is the crown jewel and the last of the Class III+ rapids of the run. It is a standing wave about as tall as the boats are long. It is caused by the 1500 cubic feet/second current folding in on itself, suddenly reduced to about 30' wide as it drops into a gorge. People, including photographers with expensive equipment, will walk down from the highway to sit on the rocks and watch the rafters on this rapid.

Failure on Hospital Bar is not painful, but it is humiliating: If you are not in the right place at the right orientation and at the right speed, you will miss it, and end up in an eddy on the left bank that fits just one boat. There is no forgiveness: This location is known as "The Parking Lot." It usually means you will sit in it and watch the next several boats pass by—your boat becoming both a warning for others of what not to do and a bumper pad so that their miscue is not as bad as yours. The Parking Lot is rock-lined on the down-stream sides and the water there is only about 15" deep. Yes, we got stuck in it—but we learned from it: Paddling upstream and out of it is a near impossibility, unless you happen to have a boat full of would-be guides, and extrication in this manner elicits an enormous cheer from the rock-bound audience. The normal resolution is that the crew becomes waders, tossing the boat over the downstream rocks and re-boarding. In either case, when you finally do get out of the Parking Lot, you have missed Hospital Bar. Though you can almost touch it with the end of a paddle, you are downstream and in a gorge. If you really want it, then plan another trip.

On the other hand, if you manage to hit Hospital Bar just right—and even and especially if you happen to air-launch a "swimmer" or two along way—you will be talking about a certain rapid for the rest of the trip, the drive home and at church the next day.

The method for proper passage is not intuitive: If you simply aim for the middle, be sure to get your parking validated. The way I learned it, you need to be about 1 boat-width to the right of the center, have a good paddle speed right up to the lead edge of the wave (where your paddlers will naturally stop paddling anyway) and then make every effort to steer the nose right to about the 2 o'clock position. Perhaps there are other ways, but I know this way for the usual reasons: 1) someone showed me, and 2) from my own successes and failures in the venture.

So, what does the apex of the gorge-run of the South Fork have to do with the study of *The Book of Mormon*? (A river guide in training will tell you white-water rafting has something to do with everything.) We "figure out for ourselves" many things in our lives only because someone points us in the right direction.

I have read *The Book of Mormon* dozens of times. I've studied it most of my lifetime—certainly more than I have studied any other text. I have done so because I enjoy the opportunity to learn from it continually. And yet I have often felt I spend a certain amount of the time in the Parking Lot, looking over at Hospital Bar. Believing:

> **Doctrine and Covenants 20:8-9**
>
> **8** ...The Book of Mormon;
>
> **9** Which contains...the fulness of the gospel of Jesus Christ...

—But not initially finding all of the components of the gospel in it. Dreaming of an understanding, for example, of those chapters of Isaiah just as Elder Bruce R. McConkie, an apostle in this dispensation has encouraged us to strive for, but having it just out of reach—again. Isaiah's words must be important if the Son of God, would quote the ancient prophet to the Nephites instead of simply stating the facts.

> **(See 3 Nephi 22, compare Isaiah 54)**

And a co-testifier of its import is its inclusion by Mormon, the editor, noting in

> **3 Nephi 26:6**
>
> **6**...there cannot be written in this book even a hundredth part of the things which Jesus did truly teach unto the people...

Yet Mormon opted to include a particular chapter of Isaiah instead? And:

> **2 Nephi 31:20**
>
> **20** ...Wherefore, if ye shall press forward, feasting upon the word of Christ, and endure to the end, Behold thus saith the Father: Ye shall have eternal life."

If the scriptures are supposed to be a smorgasbord why do I sometimes feel I am partitioned from the "produce"?

And finally—right after sharing hundreds of verses of some of the least-understood ancient scripture—Nephi writes:

> **2 Nephi 25:4**
>
> **4**…my soul delighteth in plainness unto my people, that they may learn.

It seems to me there are some parts that are not intuitive….

In the area where I live, feral pigs have mixed with Russian boars imported a century ago. Hunters will often bring their kill to a local butcher specializing in wild game and usually they will ask to save the tenderloin and make sausage with the rest. The very best part is saved for special cooking, none of the meat is wasted, and making sausage allows for enough spices to make even the gamiest meat palatable.

What if we were to butcher a nice grain-fed beef the same way? What if we were to take the tenderloins and grind the rest into hamburger? Again, in this way the best part is saved for special cooking, none of the meat is (technically) wasted, and grinding hamburger is uncomplicated.

But it does not happen: A modern butcher understands the anatomy of the cow, and instead cuts it into sections the consumer can really appreciate: Ribeye, T-bone, porterhouse and sirloin steaks, the tri-tip, brisket, flank, and short-ribs. Much care goes into raising a beef. And because of it, from internationally renowned chefs to the weekend barbeque-er we continue to learn ways of cooking each cut to enhance flavor and improve the savory experience.

The Book of Mormon is like a beef cow. How much of it are we just grinding? Greater understanding of the anatomy or structure of *The Book of Mormon* will afford us greater admiration of and comprehension of the meat of the doctrine.

16 And it shall come to pass, that whoso repenteth and is baptized in my name shall be filled; and if he endureth to the end, behold, him will I hold guiltless before my Father at that day when I shall stand to judge the world.

19 And no unclean thing can enter into his kingdom; therefore nothing entereth into his rest save it be those who have washed their garments in my blood, because of their faith, and the repentance of all their sins, and their faithfulness unto the end.

20 Now this is the commandment: Repent, all ye ends of the earth, and come unto me and be baptized in my name, that ye may be sanctified by the reception of the Holy Ghost, that ye may stand spotless before me at the last day.

21Verily, verily, I say unto you, this is my gospel...

This indicates a first target audience of the writers of *The Book of Mormon* were those who were at a state in their lives when they needed to find the path of the gospel of Jesus Christ, and to believe in Him.

As believers, we are encouraged to read and study *The Book of Mormon* and other scripture. Certainly, one of the reasons is that we continue in our journey to "come unto Christ". Nephi wrote:

2 Nephi 31:19

19 And now, my beloved brethren, after ye have gotten into this strait and narrow path, I would ask if all is done? Behold, I say unto you, Nay; ...

I would like to demonstrate that there was a second target audience Nephi was particularly writing to: This group was already in the path.

Tracts of forest are routinely logged off completely and then replanted. Years go by and the trees mature. From ground level, they appear to be a common forest. However, from a view from an airplane, patterns in the placement of the plants can be seen. I would like to describe a similar approach to the study of *The Book of Mormon*. This bird's-eye view approach is a useful tool to learning, and you may already be using it.

There is an enhanced version of the "bird's-eye view" that I would like to discuss. I will call it a "macro-view", and define it as follows: A process of scripture study in which all details of the work are considered important and part of the pandect. The plan would be that none are skipped over. A macro-view is one's mental creation of a matrix or model in which we can place various details of the scripture with commonalities in association with one another. This matrix has some benefits which will be demonstrated in this volume:

1) It permits us to see patterns in the details that allow us some insight into the thinking of the editors of *The Book of Mormon*. We will gain an appreciation of the abstracts prepared both by the writers and by the editors of *The Book of Mormon* by beginning perhaps—in some small way—to reconstruct them. We will begin to see the effort and genius of their work.

2) Like a jigsaw puzzle, the matrix creates open spaces which will direct us in the discovery of pieces that we might at first have overlooked.

3) Just as a stone arch becomes stable only when those last few pieces are inserted, a new understanding of the lessons from the editors of *The Book of Mormon* and a greater testimony as to its

truthfulness are attained as we discover that all of these details had purpose.

4) Through this analytical process, we can create an avenue in which ancient prophet-editors can minister to us in ways that they had intended, but perhaps we were not previously prepared for.

This method of study is different than the perhaps more common study method of extracting doctrinal verses from the context in order to study them singly. In *The Book of Mormon* there are overarching concepts authors planned for and intended in addition to the points of doctrine. They are most easily realized when the context is understood, and this starts with the reading of the entire story—which may last several verses, several chapters, or even a few books within *The Book of Mormon*. The issue creating a possible blind-spot is that we often read it—well—like scripture. Meaning we do not often read it all in one sitting, we refer to it in small sound-bites of verses, and perhaps are sometimes a bit myopic in our study, attempting to rend the last marrow of meaning from the word or phrase wrested between our thumbs on the page. I am not saying we can't gain much great and treasurable understanding and knowledge from these practices—including perhaps even more meaning than the original author had intended. (More on this point soon). A "macro-view" approach should not be regarded as a return to the way a novel is read, nor should it replace any of the study processes you are currently employing. The desired effect is that it should enhance them.

I intend to demonstrate there is also much to gain by a reading of *The Book of Mormon* by reading it from an enhanced arms-length prospective so to speak, so that not only the storyline, but the over-arching principles will also become more visible.

This method of analysis is possible with *The Book of Mormon* more so than with *The Bible* because *The Book of Mormon* has not been through as many translation-filters. Unlike *The Bible*, *The Book of Mormon* was translated from original reformed Egyptian into King James-Biblical English one time, and by a prophet of God who was called by God to that specific work. Because of the additional trust in the finer points that this brief custody-chain allows us, we can confidently examine the details and determine their particular positions as building blocks of the lattice of the lessons intended by the editors.

You might think such an overviewing would have a tendency to miss fines and subtleties in the scripture, but as it turns out, the opposite is true. The added "macro-view" approach tends to position and highlight many details that otherwise may seem insignificant.

Two quick examples:

The first is algebra: If you are given a single equation with multiple unknown factors, it is usually unsolvable. However, if you are given several equations with the same variables and a similar structure, then by using methods of matrices and determinants it is usually possible to solve for all of the unknowns. Instead of skipping over the smaller details, we can use them as additional equations for the matrix.

The second is Sudoku: Sudoku is a game composed of a square matrix of 81 spaces, wherein the numbers 1 through 9 are placed such that each may appear only once in each horizontal line, once in each vertical line and once in each of the 3x3 sub-matrices. Some of the numbers are placed to set the board. A pencil with an eraser is a good way to start. If one were to see a bunch of single integers jumbled on a desk, one may not guess right off they were—or could be—puzzle pieces. But that is exactly how Sudoku treats them.

The same is true with many of the perhaps lesser details of *The Book of Mormon*. Many of the pieces are already in place. The awareness of a bird's-eye view and the mental creation of a matrix will help us arrange these lesser details into their place in the picture. There is some repeat since many of the details are pieces of multiple lessons, which we recognize as further authentication of the work. There are lessons to be learned from these details.

As mentioned, there are times when we glean more meaning from the scriptures than appears to be originally intended by the author. Usually this practice is lauded as a part of likening the scriptures unto ourselves. Likening the scriptures unto ourselves is important. However, I would point out that there are instances where modification of the teaching in the scripture to suit the circumstance of the reader can mask the original lesson. This is most commonly done when a verse, or two are taken out of context in such a way that the small lesson is understood, but at the expense of the broader, originally intended instruction. For example:

2 Nephi 31:5

5 And now, if the Lamb of God, he being holy, should have need to be baptized by water, to fulfil all righteousness, O then, how much more need have we, being unholy, to be baptized, yea, even by water!

And

Ether 12:27

27 And if men come unto me I will show unto them their weakness. I give unto men weakness that they may be humble; and my grace is sufficient for all men that humble themselves before me; for if they humble themselves before me, and have faith in me, then will I make weak things become strong unto them.

Both of these verses are well-known simple, sound-bite lessons in and of themselves, but we will examine how they can outshine the instruction that they are a subsection of, such that the greater lesson—and frankly the reason that the author originally wrote it—has become unfamiliar.

Though I have attached the name "macro-view" to this study process, I have been and will be intentionally vague about how each of us might create a macro-view matrix, flowchart or spreadsheet in order to define the relationships between the details. I've named it and will refer to it by this name to encourage you to try a study pattern of *The Book of Mormon* that you probably already tried before in some measure. Go all-in and experiment for one full reading. In order to do so, it is necessary that details should be taken primarily in context, mostly at face value, and from a viewpoint that is unobstructed even by those simpler lessons. I believe that if we separate the author's original intent from the act of likening it unto ourselves that we will be able to see the scriptures from the editor's perspective and thereby be in a better position to—at that point—liken these scriptures unto ourselves.

CHAPTER 5

Guidance From Ancients

F ive chapters in Alma illustrate an overarching lesson from Mormon the editor.

One could be forgiven for questioning whether shedding light of this perspective is helpful before one has had the chance to read *The Book of Mormon*, at least a few times. Let me give you one example to explain why this might not be true: Alma, Chapter 30, speaks of Korihor, who was antichrist:

Alma 30:12

12 And this Anti-Christ, whose name was Korihor, (and the law could have no hold upon him) began to preach unto the people that there should be no Christ.

Then Chapter 31 tells of the Zoramites, who were antichrist.

Alma 31:8

18 Now the Zoramites were dissenters from the Nephites...

And mentions their repeated prayer:

Alma 31:16

16...we believe that thou hast separated us from our brethren; and we do not believe in the tradition of our brethren, which was handed down to them by the childishness of their fathers; but we believe that thou hast elected us to be thy holy children; and also thou hast made it known unto us that there shall be no Christ."

One might question the need for these verses as part of the literary composition of *The Book of Mormon*, especially if, according to its title page, it is intended to help the student to come unto Jesus Christ.

The Book of Mormon, **Title page:**

"...to the convincing of the Jew and Gentile that Jesus is the Christ, the Eternal God.

But then the next chapter is a brilliant sermon describing the abstract concept of faith, especially at its tender beginnings, and offering a way for one to test it for oneself. Faith is like a seed.

Alma 32:28 (See also verses 26-27, 29-33)

28 Now, we will compare the word unto a seed. Now, if ye give place, that a seed may be planted in your heart, behold, if it be a true seed, or a good seed, if ye do not cast it out by your unbelief, that ye will resist the Spirit of the Lord, behold, it will begin to swell within your breasts; and when you feel these swelling motions, ye will begin to say within yourselves—It must needs be that this is a good seed, or that the word is good, for it beginneth to enlarge my soul; yea, it beginneth to enlighten my understanding, yea, it beginneth to be delicious to me.

Then the next two chapters reinforce this with the testimony of ancient prophets, Zenos:

Alma 33:11

11 And thou didst hear me because of mine afflictions and my sincerity; and it is because of thy Son that thou hast been thus merciful unto me, therefore I will cry unto thee in all mine afflictions, for in thee is my joy; for thou hast turned thy judgments away from me, because of thy Son.

And Zenock:

Alma 33:16

16 For behold, he said: Thou art angry, O Lord, with this people, because they will not understand thy mercies which thou hast bestowed upon them because of thy Son.

And, as if that isn't enough, there is the testimony of the law of Moses and it's pointing to the Savior.

Alma 34:13-16 (See also verses 11-12)

13 Therefore, it is expedient that there should be a great and last sacrifice, and then shall there be, or it is expedient there should be, a stop to the shedding of blood; then shall the law of Moses be fulfilled; yea, it shall be all fulfilled, every jot and tittle, and none shall have passed away.

14 And behold, this is the whole meaning of the law, every whit pointing to that great and last sacrifice; and that great and last sacrifice will be the Son of God, yea, infinite and eternal.

15 And thus he shall bring salvation to all those who shall believe on his name; this being the intent of this last sacrifice, to bring about the bowels of mercy, which overpowereth justice, and bringeth about means unto men that they may have faith unto repentance.

16 And thus mercy can satisfy the demands of justice, and encircles them in the arms of safety, while he that exercises no faith unto repentance is exposed to the whole law of the demands of justice; therefore only unto him that has faith unto repentance is brought about the great and eternal plan of redemption.

The result is we learn that Mormon—the editor who lived centuries later—masterfully abridged the history to include this five-chapter lesson for the benefit of those in our dispensation. This template is not visible if the reader is reading only on a fine-detail level. In such a case, one can indeed miss the forest for the trees. The addition of an enhanced bird's-eye view approach allows the reader to see the pattern designed by the editor, and then understand that he intentionally extracted and distilled these things from the many records that were available to him from that time period for inclusion in *The Book of Mormon*.

CHAPTER 6

Purpose of a Prophet

With the pursuit of the editor's purposes in mind, let us skip to a moment in history that occurred many hundreds of years prior to Mormon, and introduce another macro-view matrix:

> **Ether 2:14**
>
> 14 ...And for the space of three hours did the Lord talk with the brother of Jared, and chastened him because he remembered not to call upon the name of the Lord.

Those two lines might be the soundbite/highlight of this particular story of the life of the brother of Jared. And its message: Pray. A good lesson for us: We should pray. However, these anecdotes are sometimes like parables, in the sense there may be multiple levels of learning.

If one were to examine further, was the brother of Jared chastised by the Lord for simply not praying? The brother of Jared, who was:

1. A prophet of God, and known as one who prayed:

Ether 1:34-40

34 And the brother of Jared being a large and mighty man, and a man highly favored of the Lord, Jared, his brother, said unto him: Cry unto the Lord, that he will not confound us that we may not understand our words.

35 And it came to pass that the brother of Jared did cry unto the Lord, and the Lord had compassion upon Jared; therefore he did not confound the language of Jared; and Jared and his brother were not confounded.

36 Then Jared said unto his brother: Cry again unto the Lord, and it may be that he will turn away his anger from them who are our friends, that he confound not their language.

37 And it came to pass that the brother of Jared did cry unto the Lord, and the Lord had compassion upon their friends and their families also, that they were not confounded.

38 And it came to pass that Jared spake again unto his brother, saying: Go and inquire of the Lord whether he will drive us out of the land, and if he will drive us out of the land, cry unto him whither we shall go. And who knoweth but the Lord will carry us forth into a land which is choice above all the earth? And if it so be, let us be faithful unto the Lord, that we may receive it for our inheritance.

39 And it came to pass that the brother of Jared did cry unto the Lord according to that which had been spoken by the mouth of Jared.

40 And it came to pass that the Lord did hear the brother of Jared, and had compassion upon him...

2. Not long after this, he was commended by the Lord as one who has such faith as had not been known upon the earth.

> **Ether 3: 9-12**
>
> **9** And the Lord said unto him: Because of thy faith thou hast seen that I shall take upon me flesh and blood; and never has man come before me with such exceeding faith as thou hast; for were it not so ye could not have seen my finger. Sawest thou more than this?
>
> **10** And he answered: Nay; Lord, show thyself unto me.
>
> **11** And the Lord said unto him: Believest thou the words which I shall speak?
>
> **12** And he answered: Yea, Lord, I know that thou speakest the truth, for thou art a God of truth, and canst not lie.

By virtue of such faith, he could not be kept within the veil, but would see the Lord Himself, as well as the entire history of the world.

> **Ether 3: 13-14, 17-18, 25**
>
> **13** And when he had said these words, behold, the Lord showed himself unto him, and said: Because thou knowest these things ye are redeemed from the fall; therefore ye are brought back into my presence; therefore I show myself unto you.
>
> **14** Behold, I am he who was prepared from the foundation of the world to redeem my people. Behold, I am Jesus Christ.
>
> **17** And now, as I, Moroni, said I could not make a full account of these things which are written, therefore it sufficeth me to say that Jesus showed himself unto this

man in the spirit, even after the manner and in the likeness of the same body even as he showed himself unto the Nephites.

18 And he ministered unto him even as he ministered unto the Nephites; and all this, that this man might know that he was God, because of the many great works which the Lord had showed unto him.

25 And when the Lord had said these words, he showed unto the brother of Jared all the inhabitants of the earth which had been, and also all that would be; and he withheld them not from his sight, even unto the ends of the earth.

It is inconceivable that someone without the faith to pray just days before would have enough faith to receive, such that:

Ether 3:19

19...he knew, nothing doubting.

He was summarily redeemed from the fall. He was permitted to see the history of the world. He was shown all things. (Ether 3:26)

Indeed, if he was simply not praying, then what is the message to us? Are we not commanded to pray? Should we not pray to demonstrate faith? Why have we not received as he did?

3. The Lord spoke to the brother of Jared.

Ether 2:14

14 And it came to pass at the end of four years that the Lord came again unto the brother of Jared, and stood in a cloud and talked with him. And for the space of three

hours did the Lord talk with the brother of Jared, and chastened him because he remembered not to call upon the name of the Lord.

Not only did the Lord speak to the brother of Jared, He "chastened *him* because *he* remembered not to call upon the name of the Lord." This chastening was personal and specific. If the Lord were chastening the brother of Jared for simply not praying—discounting the incongruous alternatives including that the brother of Jared was the only one of the Jaredites who was not praying, or that the brother of Jared was the only one in the group who was qualified to pray——then it would seem the Lord would have chastened all of the Jaredites through his prophet, as has been his practice before and since, certainly documented in other scripture.

2 Nephi 32:8

8 ...it grieveth me that I must speak concerning this thing. For if ye would hearken unto the Spirit which teacheth a man to pray, ye would know that ye must pray; for the evil teacheth not a man to pray, but teacheth him that he must not pray.

3 Nephi 18:17-21

17 And it came to pass that when Jesus had spoken these words unto his disciples, he turned again unto the multitude and said unto them:

18 Behold, verily, verily, I say unto you, ye must watch and pray always lest ye enter into temptation; for Satan desireth to have you, that he may sift you as wheat.

19 Therefore ye must always pray unto the Father in my name;

> **20** And whatsoever ye shall ask the Father in my name, which is right, believing that ye shall receive, behold it shall be given unto you.
>
> **21** Pray in your families unto the Father, always in my name, that your wives and your children may be blessed.

The other possibility is that "... call(ing) on the name of the Lord" is not synonymous with praying. It would seem to call it praying is an oversimplification. If we look at the entire incident, there are indications of another definition.

Let us go back to time of the tower, when Jared asks his brother—whom he recognized as the prophet of God—to ask God to not confound the language of his family:

> **Ether 1:34-35**
>
> **34** And the brother of Jared being a large and mighty man, and a man highly favored of the Lord, Jared, his brother, said unto him: Cry unto the Lord, that he will not confound us that we may not understand our words.
>
> **35** And it came to pass that the brother of Jared did cry unto the Lord, and the Lord had compassion upon Jared; therefore he did not confound the language of Jared; and Jared and his brother were not confounded.

The brother of Jared does so, and God does not confound the language of their families. Then Jared asks his brother to ask God to not confound the language of their friends:

Ether 1:36-37

36 Then Jared said unto his brother: Cry again unto the Lord, and it may be that he will turn away his anger from them who are our friends, that he confound not their language.

37 And it came to pass that the brother of Jared did cry unto the Lord, and the Lord had compassion upon their friends and their families also, that they were not confounded.

And the brother of Jared does so, and the Lord allowed the language of their friends to not be confounded. Next, Jared asks his brother to inquire about the possibility of leaving the area of Babel, perhaps to a better land.

Ether 1:38-43

38 And it came to pass that Jared spake again unto his brother, saying: Go and inquire of the Lord whether he will drive us out of the land, and if he will drive us out of the land, cry unto him whither we shall go. And who knoweth but the Lord will carry us forth into a land which is choice above all the earth? And if it so be, let us be faithful unto the Lord, that we may receive it for our inheritance.

39 And it came to pass that the brother of Jared did cry unto the Lord according to that which had been spoken by the mouth of Jared.

40 And it came to pass that the Lord did hear the brother of Jared, and had compassion upon him, and said unto him:

41 Go to and gather together thy flocks, both male and female, of every kind; and also of the seed of the earth of

> every kind; and thy families; and also Jared thy brother and his family; and also thy friends and their families, and the friends of Jared and their families.
>
> 42 And when thou hast done this thou shalt go at the head of them down into the valley which is northward. And there will I meet thee, and I will go before thee into a land which is choice above all the lands of the earth.

The brother of Jared does so, and the Lord tells them he will indeed take them to a choice land. And then the Lord promises them a great blessing when they arrive at that choice land.

> **Ether 1:43**
>
> 43 And there will I bless thee and thy seed, and raise up unto me of thy seed, and of the seed of thy brother, and they who shall go with thee, a great nation. And there shall be none greater than the nation which I will raise up unto me of thy seed, upon all the face of the earth.

And he tells them why he gives them this great blessing.

> **Ether 1:43**
>
> 43...And thus I will do unto thee because this long time ye have cried unto me.

He directs them out of the land of Babel, and they move to the seashore, where they live not in a choice land, but at least it is beach-front property. And they stay there, living in their tents. For. Four. Years.

> **Ether 2:13**
>
> **13**...they called the name of the place Moriancumer; and they dwelt in tents, and dwelt in tents upon the seashore for the space of four years.

There's the issue: Four years of beach-side bliss.

> **Ether 2:14**
>
> **14** And it came to pass at the end of four years that the Lord came again unto the brother of Jared, and stood in a cloud and talked with him. And for the space of three hours did the Lord talk with the brother of Jared, and chastened him because he remembered not to call upon the name of the Lord.

It seems that the chastisement from the Lord had to do with his particular calling and with his action below his potential. It seems to follow the narrative that because it was his calling as the prophet to receive revelation for the group, therefore inherent in this calling was the responsibility to *call upon the name of the Lord to ask for revelation*—and it follows with chastisement because he was not doing so. He was waiting for four years for the Lord to give him revelation—-which in this case was that he should build ships and push into the sea toward the Promised Land—when he had not put forth the requisite effort. Even though it was the same sort of effort that he had put forth in documented cases that had blessed him and his people to get as far as they had. This effort in studying it out in one's mind and asking of God in prayer was and is an important demonstration of faith, such that God can grant the inquisitor and his people the blessings needed without hampering their agency by giving them truth prior to faith.

What was true in the day of the brother of Jared, was true in the day of Oliver Cowdery:

> **Doctrine and Covenants 9:7-8**
>
> **7** Behold, you have not understood; you have supposed that I would give it unto you, when you took no thought save it was to ask me.
>
> **8** But, behold, I say unto you, that you must study it out in your mind; then you must ask me if it be right, and if it is right I will cause that your bosom shall burn within you; therefore, you shall feel that it is right.

In the case of the brother of Jared, it appears he neither studied it out, nor asked. But all was not lost.

> **Ether 2:15**
>
> **15** And the brother of Jared repented of the evil which he had done, and did call upon the name of the Lord for his brethren who were with him. And the Lord said unto him: I will forgive thee and thy brethren of their sins...

This is not simply doubling down on the idea that a prophet of God forgot to pray: He had sinned because he had greater understanding and greater light and had not lived according to the greater light—which in this case was to ask for and to receive revelation. Also, in mentioning he "did call upon the name of the Lord for his brethren who were with him" indicates an indictment of Jared, who thrice demonstrated that he had a good thing going in being inspired with ideas and then having his brother, the prophet, take them to the Lord. And yet this activity seemed to stop when they reached the relative safety and security of the seashore.

In retrospect, it is clear that God had a plan for the Jaredites, and God had a prophet who had great faith even though he and his people got side-tracked for a few years. God was patient and waited for a prophet to understand his role well enough that said prophet would not only ask about the plan for his people, but also inquire about how to implement it.

With this in mind, we understand then the chastening was more likely a reviewing of how to do his calling properly. In that way, when in a subsequent chapter it is recorded that the brother of Jared asked about lights on the barges, the Lord left it up to the brother of Jared to solve, giving him the opportunity to act according to his recent training:

Ether 2:21-25

21 And it came to pass that the brother of Jared did so, according as the Lord had commanded.

22 And he cried again unto the Lord saying: O Lord, behold I have done even as thou hast commanded me; and I have prepared the vessels for my people, and behold there is no light in them. Behold, O Lord, wilt thou suffer that we shall cross this great water in darkness?

23 And the Lord said unto the brother of Jared: What will ye that I should do that ye may have light in your vessels? For behold, ye cannot have windows, for they will be dashed in pieces; neither shall ye take fire with you, for ye shall not go by the light of fire.

24 For behold, ye shall be as a whale in the midst of the sea; for the mountain waves shall dash upon you. Nevertheless, I will bring you up again out of the depths of the sea; for the winds have gone forth out of my mouth, and also the rains and the floods have I sent forth.

25 And behold, I prepare you against these things; for ye cannot cross this great deep save I prepare you against the waves of the sea, and the winds which have gone forth, and the floods which shall come. Therefore what will ye that I should prepare for you that ye may have light when ye are swallowed up in the depths of the sea?

And the Lord said, "What would you have me do?" The brother of Jared was given the opportunity to put into practice what he had learned during the undocumented "chastisement," and devise a plan—probably based on at least one previous similar incident in his known scripture:

Genesis 6:13, 16

13 And God said unto Noah…

16 A window shalt thou make to the ark…

LDS footnote to Genesis 6:16

HEB *toshar;* some rabbis believe that it was a precious stone that shone in the ark.

So this might have inspired the idea, but he would not return to the Lord with just an idea…

Ether 3:1

1 And it came to pass that the brother of Jared, (now the number of the vessels which had been prepared was eight) went forth unto the mount, which they called the mount Shelem, because of its exceeding height, and did molten out of a rock sixteen small stones; and they were white

> and clear, even as transparent glass; and he did carry them in his hands upon the top of the mount, and cried again unto the Lord....

He not only prepared stones, which had to have been quite a process, but he then carried them up to the top of the high mountain. In the end, he brought

a. The inspired idea, gleaned from his knowledge of the history of God's dealings with his people;

b. The effort/sweat-equity: doing his part to make it happen, in this case to build a fire, bellows, etc. to molten the stones;

c. The effort of climbing up to the top of the mountain;

d. The effort of carrying these stones up to the top of the mountain;

And also:

e. His faith in the Lord, trusting in the lesson that the Lord had taught him;

f. His faith that the Lord could do anything; and

g. His faith that the Lord would help them.

Ether 3:4-6

4 And I know, O Lord, that thou hast all power, and can do whatsoever thou wilt for the benefit of man; therefore touch these stones, O Lord, with thy finger, and prepare them that they may shine forth in darkness; and they shall shine forth unto us in the vessels which we have prepared, that we may have light while we shall cross the sea.

> **5** Behold, O Lord, thou canst do this. We know that thou art able to show forth great power, which looks small unto the understanding of men.
>
> **6** And it came to pass that when the brother of Jared had said these words, behold, the Lord stretched forth his hand and touched the stones one by one with his finger.

There are a few points that we learn from this experience:

1. Being a prophet is hard work. And we're not talking about just getting God's message to the people. The Lord requires significant effort in the demonstration of faith, even from his prophets.

2. In considering this plan in the first place, the brother of Jared must have thought about the benefit of the lights being a sign to the people to maintain their faith and to not fear—not only in boarding the barges but in the many months of travel in them.

3. What would the brother of Jared have learned about himself if, in response to his query, the Lord had simply said, "I'll just put a pair of glowing stones in each of your barges," and done so?

4. The response to this request to the Lord made by the brother of Jared was not verbal. It was recorded as immediate action: *The Lord stretched forth his hand,* which was another teaching moment to the brother of Jared—and to us.

Also, it is interesting to note that the receipt of the specific blessing requested by the brother of Jared—which was that the stones should "shine forth in the darkness"—is not even recorded by Moroni until sometime later:

Do we pray for "thy kingdom come" and yet hope to stay in our relatively comfortable, beach-side "Moriancumer village?" Does God want to direct and even drive us to the Promised Land, but are we as a people yet unwilling, unprepared or otherwise lack the faith to both receive act upon his council? How long before the driving force begins and the unprepared are left on the sand? How much easier to assuage the terrors of the journey when our faith and trust is in Him who makes the wind blow?

It is not meet that we should be commanded in all things.

In 1979, President Russel M. Nelson, President of The Church of Jesus Christ of Latter-day Saints was then the General President of the Sunday School of the church and was invited as a guest to the Regional Representative's seminar, to which audience President Spencer W. Kimball, then President of the Church, gave an address in which he spoke about opening the nations that were currently closed to the church.

> **Church News. November 3, 2015. Church of Jesus Christ of Latter-day Saints. "President Nelson Honored as "Old Friend" by Chinese Doctors He Trained." By Tad Walch**
>
> President Spencer W. Kimball challenged General Authorities and general officers of the faith to learn Mandarin. President Nelson...accepted President Kimball's charge and hired a tutor.

President Nelson decided to heed the word of the prophet. *He* decided to do so. President Kimball did not compel, did not tell him directly "Russell Nelson, you are to learn Chinese—now." Instead he was given the opportunity to decide to heed the counsel. And I would think that he was blessed in his learning of it. Great opportunities and blessings were given to him to draw nearer to the Chinese people because he decided and acted.

A friend of mine had a church calling wherein he was given a directive from his leader that he should do a couple of things. His understanding was not that he *had* to do them, but that he should. The things that he was directed to do were difficult for a variety of reasons. He asked me what I thought, and I looked at the emailed directive, along with the accompanying documentation from this leader's leader, and determined that pretty much everyone up-line said that these things needed to be implemented on my friend's level. I advised him to do it. I recommended that he should encourage all those in his sphere of influence that they too should be "anxiously engaged" in following this directive. And it turns out that a few of his colleagues already were.

I have thought about why my friend's leader gave the directive in such a way so as to allow a way out of its implementation. The Lord has said:

Doctrine and Covenants 58:26-28

26 For behold, it is not meet that I should command in all things; for he that is compelled in all things, the same is a slothful and not a wise servant; wherefore he receiveth no reward.

27 Verily I say, men should be anxiously engaged in a good cause, and do many things of their own free will, and bring to pass much righteousness;

28 For the power is in them, wherein they are agents unto themselves. And inasmuch as men do good they shall in nowise lose their reward.

It appears that the "reward" mentioned is not only speaking of the great reward on the horizon, but that there is a reward that is much more immediate: Revelation is a reward. Revelation is a blessing. The brother of Jared was "chastened" or instructed by the Lord that he needed to seek revelation in the matter of progressing to the Promised Land. Though a prophet of God—and one whose faith the Lord gave the highest praise—he was not entitled to the revelation that his people needed in order to progress until he decided to asked for it. Four years of relative ease on the beach, and yet they were the ones preventing themselves from continuing their journey to an even better place.

President Nelson was blessed when he *chose* to heed the challenge of President Kimball. It appears that my friend's leader intentionally gave the directive in such a way that my friend had agency to choose to do it or not. Our decisions determine our direction and destiny. This leader gave my friend and his associates the opportunity to choose to do it and by that choice then have the right to ask for the blessing of revelation to be able to accomplish the difficult task.

> ### Doctrine and Covenants 130:21
>
> 21 And when we obtain any blessing from God, it is by obedience to that law upon which it is predicated.

We should remember that the opposite is also true. As leading others:

> ### Doctrine and Covenants 121:36-37
>
> 36 That the rights of the priesthood are inseparably connected with the powers of heaven, and that the powers of heaven cannot be controlled nor handled only upon the principles of righteousness.

37 That they may be conferred upon us, it is true; but when we undertake to…exercise control or compulsion upon the souls of the children of men, in any degree of unrighteousness, behold, the heavens withdraw themselves; the Spirit of the Lord is grieved; and when it is withdrawn, Amen to the priesthood or the authority of that man.

Denying someone the opportunity to choose and therefore be entitled to the blessing of revelation if they request, is often—in fact—a degree of unrighteousness.

Also, as we lead ourselves and others, we should not expect revelation to accomplish the task (a) that we need be compelled to do, (b) for which we seek only to be minimally compliant, or (c) if we are not "anxiously engaged". Nor should we expect it (d) without praying for it, presenting before the Lord the requisite thought and effort in the matter.

As celestial beings, our work and our glory will be in alignment with the will of God, because it will also be His work and His glory. For this reason, it follows that we will all eventually need to learn to receive and recognize revelation. We have been given the great blessing of the opportunity to learn to receive the will of God here in mortality. To do so, we must choose to initiate the process.

Those are just a couple of examples. It is not the intention of this writer to identify an exhaustive list of macro-view "matrices" based upon a study of *The Book of Mormon*, let alone construct them, but I recommend the technique to you. The "macro view" is just a process, it is just the vine for the fruit. We will use these macro-views to re-explore some areas of *The Book of Mormon* which will help us to better understand the minds and hearts of the editors of *The Book of Mormon* as they took up the labor of creating this record for us today.

We are and must be open to the reality that more can be learned from the scriptures than is limited by the original intent of the authors/compilers/editors, but at the same time recognize that an important component of learning is to clearly understand original intent.

CHAPTER 7

Logic of Faith

When I was just four years old, I was fitted with my first pair of glasses. Upon my return home with the new look, my sisters—about 6 and 8 years old—cried. I, on the other hand, was thrilled to be able to see things more clearly than I had before.

It is not my intention to spend time to draw out any given macro-view matrix. Your view may have a different form than mine. Like the frames of glasses, they hold the lenses to see the same data in the same way. The matrix is just a tool, so we will spend more time on the function than the form. And the best way to do so is to share results.

We have become accustomed to having vast amounts of data at our fingertips. We are used to the internet housing the sum of the knowledge of mankind, and of having it sorted and readily available on our cell phones. And yet the great mystery still eludes the general public: Who is God, and what is his plan for us? The lack of skeptic-proof information on this subject has led many to conclude that either there is no God or that he does not care about us or what we do. Why—especially in this time when information is king—does mankind generally still not absolutely *know* what God wants us to do? Why the continuing mystery?

First we need to be clear on our definition of faith. The worldly view is that faith is just a placeholder until we have knowledge. Armed with this definition, an agnostic will identify "people of faith" as believing in differing ideas and therefore will conclude that probably none of it is true, because surely and logically if there is a God, he would not present himself in so many different and incongruous ways.

Joseph Smith cleared this up many years ago and yet the myth still persists, even within the church. "We strive to have the faith to be obedient so that we can go to heaven" is an oversimplification and is—in fact—missing the point.

> **Joseph Smith: Lectures on Faith, Lecture First:**
>
> 7. The author of the epistle to the Hebrews, in the eleventh chapter of that epistle and first verse, gives the following definition of faith:
>
> 8. "Now faith is the substance (assurance) of things hoped for, the evidence of things not seen."
>
> 9. From this we learn that faith is the assurance which men have of the existence of things which they have not seen, and the principle of action in all intelligent beings.
>
> 10. ...it is faith, and faith only, which is the moving cause of all action in them; that without it both mind and body would be in a state of inactivity, and all their exertions would cease, both physical and mental.
>
> 11. ...Would you have ever sown, if you had not believed that you would reap? ...In a word, is there anything that you would have done either physical or mental, if you had not previously believed?
>
> 12. And as faith is the moving cause of all actions in temporal concerns, so it is in spiritual....

13....But faith is not only the principle of action, but of power also, in all intelligent beings, whether in heaven or on earth. Thus says that author of the epistle to the Hebrews, xi.3—

14. "Through faith we understand that the worlds were framed by the word of God; so that things which were seen were not made by things which do appear."

15. By this we understand that the principle of power which existed in the bosom of God, by which the worlds were framed, was faith; and that it is by reason of this principle of power existing in the Deity, that all created things exist; so that all things in heaven, on earth, or under the earth exist by reason of faith as it existed in Him.

16. Had it not been for the principle of faith the worlds would never have been framed neither would man have been formed from the dust. It is the same principle by which Jehovah works, and through which he exercises power over all temporal as well as eternal things. Take this principle or attribute—for it is an attribute—from the Deity, and he would cease to exist.

17. Who cannot see, that if God framed the worlds by faith, that it is by faith that he exercises power over them, and that faith is the principle of power?

There is more to the development of faith than simply having enough to be obedient to return to God. In short: In order to develop to do the things that God does, we need to cultivate faith.

We are currently here on this earth, to learn to become like God.

All in the human family were spiritually born of Heavenly Parents. We are children of God.

Before our time here on earth, we lived in a premortal existence, in the presence of God.

In pre-mortality, we desired to be like God: We recognized that God had a physical body. We learned as we could, but because we didn't have physical bodies, there was a limit to our development in this area. We did have spirit bodies, and one can surmise that we had some personal development in that area. We came to earth and received physical bodies, so that we could continue to learn to develop this physical-body attribute that God has.

Likewise, in pre-mortality, we desired to be like God: We recognized that God had perfect faith. Whereas our faith is perfected in Our Lord and Savior Jesus Christ, God's faith is in Himself. (Lectures on faith, Lecture Second, questions and answers page 23.) We learned as we could, but because we were in God's presence, there was a limit to our development in this area. We, as the two-thirds of God's children who would be born into mortality in this world, had at least some personal development in this area such that we had faith in Christ—at least enough that we did not actively oppose His plan of happiness for us. We came to earth and received a forgetting of our premortal existence, so that we could continue to learn to develop this faith-attribute that God has.

Again, in pre-mortality, we desired to be like God: Just as his other attributes, God has perfect agency. God gave us agency according to our sphere and according to our understanding. And we made choices. We learned as we could, but because we were in God's presence, there was a limit to our development in this area. We came to earth and received a forgetting of our premortal existence. This was in part so that we could continue to learn to develop this agency-attribute that God has.

This veil of forgetting our previous life is a gift given to us in order that we might have the opportunity to develop faith through agency. The veil is not a curse, nor is it designed by God as an irritant any more than is the act of giving us each a physical body. These are blessings given to those who, in pre-mortality, chose to accept them and follow His plan.

Agency is a gift from God. It was given to us in pre-mortality and expands as choices expand. As we make bad choices, it shrinks and limits us into something less than our potential. The Hosanna Anthem, an arrangement of the sacred hymn "The Spirit of God" Includes the following lines:

www.churchofjesuschrist.org/study/vide/conference-music/2020-04-4061-hosanna-anthem-the-spirit-of-god-1080p?lang-eng

Thanks be to God for his eternal mercies,

Thanks be to God for endless liberty,

Thanks be to God, for endless liberty."

Lucifer's plan in the pre-existence was to take away our agency. In doing so, he would take away our ability to continue to develop faith. His plan was to force obedience so that there was no sin so that all would return to God's presence. The problem with that plan is that we would not have further developed that attribute of faith. We would be damned: forever crippled from becoming like God because we were denied the opportunity to grow. We would be unable to do things that God does, like create worlds.

Hebrews 11:3

3 Through faith we understand that the worlds were framed by the word of God, so that things which are seen were not made of things which do appear.

Although Lucifer may have other schemes, we might conjecture that the plan of Lucifer in the pre-existence was simply this: No veil. This would be simple, and easy to sell to the masses. All would remember and see God, and of course therefore no one would sin. Our mortal existence would be similar to driving on a freeway when there is a police car in the adjacent lane.

One of the reasons that we come to earth is to develop the godly attribute of faith. Sometimes we lose sight of that goal. We can be distracted into thinking that the goal is to be so blessed of God that we don't have to struggle in this life. We need to be reminded that the acquisition/development of faith is a great blessing in and of itself. I believe that we will in hindsight realize that it is greater than any temporal blessing that we could ask for. We exert our faith at the first and then we exercise our faith in our reaction to the result—be it according to our will matching God's, or sensing and acknowledging that though it may not be according to our limited view and will, that it is the mind of God. Though difficult to acknowledge when we are in the middle of it, in the end it matters less that we received the requested blessing at that particular time, than that our faith matured through the experience. We are given agency so that we have a very conscious control over this kind of personal growth.

Faith precedes the miracle. Spiritual knowledge is a miracle, so it follows that faith precedes spiritual knowledge.

Since faith precedes spiritual knowledge, we should pray to be inspired to have the words to use when we pray. For example, Jared was surely specifically inspired to ask his brother to pray for their people to not only be lead away from the tower of Babel, but to an even better land. Choose faith in God. Ask that His will be done in the matter. Know that His vantage point will always have the clearer view, and have faith in Him that He loves you and wants what is best for you.

There is another reason that knowledge does not precede faith: It is because God loves his children, and does not want a stumble to be spiritually fatal.

> **Alma 32:17-19**
>
> 17 Yea, there are many who do say: If thou wilt show unto us a sign from heaven, then we shall know of a surety; then we shall believe.
>
> 18 Now I ask, is this faith? Behold, I say unto you, Nay; for if a man knoweth a thing he hath no cause to believe, for he knoweth it.
>
> 19 And now, how much more cursed is he that knoweth the will of God and doeth it not, than he that only believeth, or only hath cause to believe, and falleth into transgression?

Knowledge of God before faith is Satan's plan. It can kill the opportunity for faith in that thing, which loss constitutes a loss of agency. Not that I am in any position to understand the will of God in all things, nor to define Him by rule from my limited perspective, but it would appear that the gift of agency to his children is held inviolate: It is what "Trekkies" would call a "prime directive."

The veil also gave us another important thing: it gave us a season to repent. If we had absolute knowledge, and sinned against it, we would be as the sons of Perdition:

2 Peter 2:20

20. For if after they have escaped the pollutions of the world through the knowledge of the Lord and Saviour Jesus Christ, they are again entangled therein, and overcome, the latter end is worse with them than the beginning.

And

2 Nephi 31:18

14 But, behold, my beloved brethren, thus came the voice of the Son unto me, saying: After ye have repented of your sins, and witnessed unto the Father that ye are willing to keep my commandments, by the baptism of water, and have received the baptism of fire and of the Holy Ghost, and can speak with a new tongue, yea, even with the tongue of angels, and after this should deny me, it would have been better for you that ye had not known me.

Faith is not just a temporary state until knowledge can take over. Moreover, knowledge after faith does not kill faith.

Alma 32: 26-34

26 Now, as I said concerning faith—that it was not a perfect knowledge—even so it is with my words. Ye cannot know of their surety at first, unto perfection, any more than faith is a perfect knowledge.

27 But behold, if ye will awake and arouse your faculties, even to an experiment upon my words, and exercise a particle of faith, yea, even if ye can no more than desire to believe, let this desire work in you, even until ye believe in a manner that ye can give place for a portion of my words.

28 Now, we will compare the word unto a seed. Now, if ye give place, that a seed may be planted in your heart, behold, if it be a true seed, or a good seed, if ye do not cast it out by your unbelief, that ye will resist the Spirit of the Lord, behold, it will begin to swell within your breasts; and when you feel these swelling motions, ye will begin to say within yourselves—It must needs be that this is a good seed, or that the word is good, for it beginneth to enlarge my soul; yea, it beginneth to enlighten my understanding, yea, it beginneth to be delicious to me.

29 Now behold, would not this increase your faith? I say unto you, Yea; nevertheless it hath not grown up to a perfect knowledge.

30 But behold, as the seed swelleth, and sprouteth, and beginneth to grow, then you must needs say that the seed is good; for behold it swelleth, and sprouteth, and beginneth to grow. And now, behold, will not this strengthen your faith? Yea, it will strengthen your faith: for ye will say I know that this is a good seed; for behold it sprouteth and beginneth to grow.

31 And now, behold, are ye sure that this is a good seed? I say unto you, Yea; for every seed bringeth forth unto its own likeness.

32 Therefore, if a seed groweth it is good, but if it groweth not, behold it is not good, therefore it is cast away.

33 And now, behold, because ye have tried the experiment, and planted the seed, and it swelleth and sprouteth, and beginneth to grow, ye must needs know that the seed is good.

34 And now, behold, is your knowledge perfect? Yea, your knowledge is perfect in that thing, and your faith is dormant; ....

"Faith is *dormant* in this thing," not dead. Faith is the foundation of the knowledge. Therefore, it stands to reason that if the faith is lost, so too is the knowledge. This is true in temporal as well as spiritual things.

To continue the analogy of the seed: Fast-forward a few years and the sprouted seed becomes a tree. A regular, vascular tree has stem and trunk made of three basic components: Xylem, phloem, and cambium.

The xylem is the middle wood, the strength and structure, and wherein moisture and nutrients are drawn from the ground.

The phloem is a sheath-like layer just inside the bark through which nutrients from the branches are fed to the roots.

The cambium is the thin layer of active plant cells between the other two. Xylem and phloem cells are essentially static. The cambium layer reproduces to build onto both the xylem and phloem. The cambium produces the rings of the tree with the changes of the season. Where there is a scion that sprouts, it is because this thin layer has produced and directed it. Cambium is responsible for all growth. Without it, the hardwood tree would have no stems, no leaves. It is the life of the tree. If the cambium layer is exposed or removed in a ring around the truck of a hardwood tree—no matter its size—that tree will die.

Knowledge is like the xylem and phloem. The hardwood of knowledge provides structure, shape, visibility, and the starting place for growth in the season of growth.

Faith is like the cambium of the tree. All increase in knowledge is from faith. Without it, as if without leaves, it could not grow with the light of the Son. Like cambium, if faith is fatally damaged, then gains turn into losses, until the entire tree of knowledge is good for nothing but to be cast into the fire.

8 And these things have I written, which are a lesser part of the things which he taught the people; and I have written them to the intent that they may be brought again unto this people, from the Gentiles, according to the words which Jesus hath spoken.

9 And when they shall have received this, *which is expedient that they should have first, to try their faith,* and if it shall so be that they shall believe these things then shall the greater things be made manifest unto them.

10 And if it so be that they will not believe these things, then shall the greater things be withheld from them, unto their condemnation.

11 Behold, I was about to write them, all which were engraven upon the plates of Nephi, but the Lord forbade it, saying: I will try the faith of my people.

This is Mormon speaking to us. The Lord did not withhold it to punish his people. Clearly the opposite is the case. To be given such knowledge makes us responsible for such knowledge and left without the ability to develop faith in this area. Hence we are to learn line by line and precept by precept. Also, such knowledge would compel us to comply, thereby denying us agency, and denying us the right to the blessing of revelation to help us accomplish the Lord's will.

Doctrine and Covenants 58:26

58 ...he that is compelled in all things, the same is a slothful and not a wise servant; wherefore he receiveth no reward.

Through the accumulation and association of many data-points on the subject, we learn more of the understanding of the ancient prophet, and why he taught us in the manner that he did. That instead of just telling us all things, he instead gave us direction so that we could continue learning by faith, so that through some effort on our part we could have access to great spiritual knowledge without inhibiting our agency.

His son, Moroni, learned and taught us this lesson again and more directly, sensing that it was important enough to interrupt his abridgement of the Jaredite record. We can get a greater feel for his depth of understanding of our need for this lesson by first following his life after the final battle through his writings.

CHAPTER 8

Moroni's Interruptions

S ometimes an analysis of the mildly pedestrian can allow passage to greater tracts of learning.

++++

To understand the writings of Moroni more fully, it is helpful to determine their chronological order. To do this we will start by using the available time-stamps:

a. Date of last great Nephite/Lamanite battle:

Mormon 6:5

5 And when three hundred and eighty and four years had passed away, we had gathered in all the remainder of our people unto the land of Cumorah.

b. Date that Moroni wrote Mormon 8.

Mormon 8:6

6 Behold, four hundred years have passed away since the coming of our Lord and Savior.

c. Date of the sealing up of the record.

> **Moroni 10:1.**
>
> 1 Now I, Moroni, write somewhat as seemeth me good; and I write unto my brethren, the Lamanites; and I would that they should know that more than four hundred and twenty years have passed away since the sign was given of the coming of Christ.

It is obvious that three dates, sixteen and twenty years apart from each other do not tell the whole story of the five or six sections of scripture engraved onto the golden plates by Moroni. Along with the time-stamps, we will explore Mormon's reasons for returning to leading the Nephite army, Mormon's literary commission, and Moroni's literary commission; we will list the known writings of Moroni—partitioning them as needed, acknowledge their content, and find instances of when one segment of his writing refers to a previous segment. This will help us determine the probable order in which the segments were written, and their order will help us to begin to understand the editor's perspective which will give us greater insights into the principles that are taught.

The brother of Jared received a great vision, showing him all the inhabitants of the earth who had been and all that would be.

> **Ether 3:17-22, 25**
>
> 17 And now, as I, Moroni, said I could not make a full account of these things which are written, therefore it sufficeth me to say that Jesus showed himself unto this man in the spirit, even after the manner and in the likeness of the same body even as he showed himself unto the Nephites.

18 And he ministered unto him even as he ministered unto the Nephites; and all this, that this man might know that he was God, because of the many great works which the Lord had showed unto him.

19 And because of the knowledge of this man he could not be kept from beholding within the veil; and he saw the finger of Jesus, which, when he saw, he fell with fear; for he knew that it was the finger of the Lord; and he had faith no longer, for he knew, nothing doubting.

20 Wherefore, having this perfect knowledge of God, he could not be kept from within the veil; therefore he saw Jesus; and he did minister unto him.

21 And it came to pass that the Lord said unto the brother of Jared: Behold, thou shalt not suffer these things which ye have seen and heard to go forth unto the world, until the time cometh that I shall glorify my name in the flesh; wherefore, ye shall treasure up the things which ye have seen and heard, and show it to no man.

22 And behold, when ye shall come unto me, ye shall write them and shall seal them up...

25 And when the Lord had said these words, he showed unto the brother of Jared all the inhabitants of the earth which had been, and also all that would be; and he withheld them not from his sight, even unto the ends of the earth.

As mentioned above, I would like to emphasis that the substance of this vision was shared with the Nephites at the time that Christ came to the Nephites.

Ether 4:1-2

1 And the Lord commanded the brother of Jared to go down out of the mount from the presence of the Lord, and write the things which he had seen; and they were forbidden to come unto the children of men until after that he should be lifted up upon the cross; and for this cause did king Mosiah keep them, that they should not come unto the world until after Christ should show himself unto his people.

2 And after Christ truly had showed himself unto his people he commanded that they should be made manifest.

Ether 3:18

18 And he ministered unto him even as he ministered unto the Nephites; and all this, that this man might know that he was God, because of the many great works which the Lord had showed unto him.

Nephi knew that the substance of the great vision of the brother of Jared would be manifest to the Nephites when Christ appeared to them.

2 Nephi 31:13

13 Wherefore, my beloved brethren, I know that if ye shall follow the Son, with full purpose of heart, acting no hypocrisy and no deception before God, but with real intent, repenting of your sins, witnessing unto the Father that ye are willing to take upon you the name of Christ, by baptism—yea, by following your Lord and your Savior down into the water, according to his word, behold, then shall ye receive the Holy Ghost; yea, then cometh the

baptism of fire and of the Holy Ghost; and then can ye speak with the tongue of angels, and shout praises unto the Holy One of Israel.

2 Nephi 32:6

6 Behold, this is the doctrine of Christ, and there will be no more doctrine given until after he shall manifest himself unto you in the flesh. And when he shall manifest himself unto you in the flesh, the things which he shall say unto you shall ye observe to do.

Nowhere in the previous several chapters is there a mention about the law of Moses, so it is safe to conclude that 2 Nephi 32:6 refers not to the old law and the fulfillment of the old law, but to the process as listed in 2 Nephi 31:13.

Mormon knew about the great vision of the brother of Jared. As mentioned previously, Mormon states:

3 Nephi 26:6-12

6 And now there cannot be written in this book even a hundredth part of the things which Jesus did truly teach unto the people;

7 But behold the plates of Nephi do contain the more part of the things which he taught the people.

8 And these things have I written, which are a lesser part of the things which he taught the people; and I have written them to the intent that they may be brought again unto this people, from the Gentiles, according to the words which Jesus hath spoken.

9And when they shall have received this, which is expedient that they should have first, to try their faith, and if it shall so be that they shall believe these things then shall the greater things be made manifest unto them.

10 And if it so be that they will not believe these things, then shall the greater things be withheld from them, unto their condemnation.

11 Behold, I was about to write them, all which were engraven upon the plates of Nephi, but the Lord forbade it, saying: I will try the faith of my people.

12 Therefore I, Mormon, do write the things which have been commanded me of the Lord. And now I, Mormon, make an end of my sayings, and proceed to write the things which have been commanded me.

From this we understand that Mormon had access to the vision of the brother of Jared as written in the (large, more historically complete) plates of Nephi. However, he was instructed not to include these "greater things" in his record.

Moroni learned a similar lesson and interrupted his abridgement of the history of the Jaredites with an account of his prayer and the answer that he received:

Ether 12:24-27

24 And thou hast made us that we could write but little, because of the awkwardness of our hands. Behold, thou hast not made us mighty in writing like unto the brother of Jared, for thou madest him that the things which he wrote were mighty even as thou art, unto the overpowering of man to read them.

25 Thou hast also made our words powerful and great, even that we cannot write them; wherefore, when we write we behold our weakness, and stumble because of the placing of our words; and I fear lest the Gentiles shall mock at our words.

26 And when I had said this, the Lord spake unto me, saying: Fools mock, but they shall mourn; and my grace is sufficient for the meek, that they shall take no advantage of your weakness;

27 And if men come unto me I will show unto them their weakness. I give unto men weakness that they may be humble; and my grace is sufficient for all men that humble themselves before me; for if they humble themselves before me, and have faith in me, then will I make weak things become strong unto them.

Moroni voiced his concern as he prayed because his words—which would be part of *The Book of Mormon*—appeared rather feeble when compared to the words of the brother of Jared. In reply he was taught that if those who receive his words are prepared, that the weakness of his words would be made strong to them. In other words, our faith would be tried, and God, in his infinite wisdom, would not punish us with the blessing of knowledge that we are not prepared for. This is different than simply saying that God will make our weaknesses to become strong, as quoting verse twenty seven out of context would imply. The latter is a good lesson by itself, but Moroni was teaching a lesson to be understood on two levels, with the latter a mere shadow of the main.

It was probably essentially the same information Nephi saw and heard when he desired to know the answers to the questions derived from his viewing of the vision of the Tree of Life, as indicated by

    a. It was a vision of a great portion of the history of the world,

1 Nephi 13:1-3

1 And it came to pass that the angel spake unto me, saying: Look! And I looked and beheld many nations and kingdoms.

2 And the angel said unto me: What beholdest thou? And I said: I behold many nations and kingdoms.

3 And he said unto me: These are the nations and kingdoms of the Gentiles.

b. The experience of Mormon is similar to the occasion when Nephi saw much of the history of the world. In this instance, Nephi was allowed to write about some of the vision, but was forbidden to write after a certain point:

1 Nephi 14:28, 30

28 And behold, I, Nephi, am forbidden that I should write the remainder of the things which I saw and heard; wherefore the things which I have written sufficeth me; and I have written but a small part of the things which I saw...

30 And now I make an end of speaking concerning the things which I saw while I was carried away in the Spirit; and if all the things which I saw are not written, the things which I have written are true. And thus it is. Amen.

c. And Nephi was told that—in this case—the apostle John would be commissioned to write it.

1 Nephi 14:18-22, 24-28, 30

18 And it came to pass that the angel spake unto me, saying: Look!

19 And I looked and beheld a man, and he was dressed in a white robe.

20 And the angel said unto me: Behold one of the twelve apostles of the Lamb.

21 Behold, he shall see and write the remainder of these things; yea, and also many things which have been.

22 And he shall also write concerning the end of the world...

24 And behold, the things which this apostle of the Lamb shall write are many things which thou hast seen; and behold, the remainder shalt thou see.

25 But the things which thou shalt see hereafter thou shalt not write; for the Lord God hath ordained the apostle of the Lamb of God that he should write them.

26 And also others who have been, to them hath he shown all things, and they have written them; and they are sealed up to come forth in their purity, according to the truth which is in the Lamb, in the own due time of the Lord, unto the house of Israel.

27 And I, Nephi, heard and bear record, that the name of the apostle of the Lamb was John, according to the word of the angel.

We note the parallelism to Mormon's experience, when he too had the information but was instructed not to include it, learning at some point that Moroni had been called to that work.

The angel told Nephi that others before him had also been shown all things:

> **1 Nephi 14:26**
>
> 26 And also others who have been, to them hath he shown all things, and they have written them; and they are sealed up to come forth in their purity, according to the truth which is in the Lamb, in the own due time of the Lord, unto the house of Israel.

One of these was the brother of Jared. This list of those who probably had access to the great vision or similar includes: The brother of Jared, Nephi, the apostle John, most likely King Mosiah—who was the seer to receive custody of the 24 golden plates found by the people of Zeniff, maybe other seer-prophets whose names are mentioned after the time of King Mosiah, and of course the Nephites of 34AD and for those few generations after. We surmise that it may be the same as Moses and/or Abraham saw, in which case, the segment recorded in *The Pearl of Great Price* might be mere glances into that grand view.

Since Mormon knew about the great vision, Mormon (and Moroni) had access to it through—if nowhere else—its recording in the Large Plates of Nephi; Mormon was given to know that he was not to include this information in *The Book of Mormon*; and Moroni was specifically directed to and did in fact engrave into gold plates the entire, unabridged great vision of the brother of Jared:

> **Ether 4:4**
>
> 4 Behold, I (Moroni) have written upon these plates the very things which the brother of Jared saw; and there never were greater things made manifest than those which were made manifest unto the brother of Jared.

Then it stands to reason, or at least it is not a great leap of imagination to understand that Mormon knew that Moroni had been called to the sacred work of scribing the great vision onto golden plates. He probably even knew that it was to be kept together on the golden plates but separate from *The Book of Mormon*.

Further support of this assumption is that if Mormon's only goal was to preserve the records and *The Book of Mormon* that he had thus-far created/compiled, then Mormon would not have returned to lead the Nephites after he had utterly refused.

Mormon 3:11, 14-16

11 And it came to pass that *I, Mormon, did utterly refuse from this time forth to be a commander and a leader of this people*, because of their wickedness and abomination.

12 Behold, I had led them, notwithstanding their wickedness I had led them many times to battle, and had loved them, according to the love of God which was in me, with all my heart; and my soul had been poured out in prayer unto my God all the day long for them; nevertheless, it was without faith, because of the hardness of their hearts.

13 And thrice have I delivered them out of the hands of their enemies, and they have repented not of their sins.

14 And when they had sworn by all that had been forbidden them by our Lord and Savior Jesus Christ, that they would go up unto their enemies to battle, and avenge themselves of the blood of their brethren, behold the voice of the Lord came unto me, saying:

15 Vengeance is mine, and I will repay; and because this people repented not after I had delivered them, behold, they shall be cut off from the face of the earth.

> **16** And it came to pass *that I utterly refused to go up against mine enemies; and I did even as the Lord had commanded me; and I did stand as an idle witness* to manifest unto the world the things which I saw and heard, according to the manifestations of the Spirit which had testified of things to come.

If this were the case, then it makes sense that it would have been safer for Mormon and for his primary commission to have continued to stand as an idle witness, protect the plates and record the carnage, just as Ether had done.

> **Ether 13:13-14**
>
> **13** ...and he hid himself in the cavity of a rock by day, *and by night he went forth viewing the things which should come upon the people.*
>
> **14** And as he dwelt in the cavity of a rock he made the remainder of this record...

But instead of hiding out and recording, or just fleeing the area to a safe place to deposit the records, he took up the cause again and agreed to lead the Nephites.

> **Mormon 5:1**
>
> **1** And it came to pass that I did go forth among the Nephites, and did repent of the oath which I had made that I would no more assist them; and they gave me command again of their armies, for they looked upon me as though I could deliver them from their afflictions.

From a careful gathering of many of additional details that might otherwise be glossed over, and comparison with the larger or more common specifics, we can gain a greater insight into the decisions that Mormon and Moroni made: the reasons that they did not follow the same action plan that the Lord had set for the earlier prophet.

At this point in his life, Mormon's goals were mostly given to him. The first was given to him as a young man:

Mormon 1:4

4 And behold, ye shall take the plates of Nephi unto yourself, and the remainder shall ye leave in the place where they are; and ye shall engrave on the plates of Nephi all the things that ye have observed concerning this people.

Ammoron's instructions were to continue the Large Plates of Nephi, the record of the kings/government of the Nephite nation. He was to scribe into them the history of the people. And Mormon indicates that he fulfilled this charge:

Mormon 2:4

18 And upon the plates of Nephi I did make a full account of all the wickedness and abominations...

The next goal was to preserve the existing records.

Mormon 4:23

23 And now I, Mormon, seeing that the Lamanites were about to overthrow the land, therefore I did go to the hill Shim, and did take up all the records which Ammaron had hid up unto the Lord.

> **Mormon 6:6**
>
> **6** And it came to pass that when we had gathered in all our people in one to the land of Cumorah, behold I, Mormon, began to be old; and knowing it to be the last struggle of my people, and having been commanded of the Lord that I should not suffer the records which had been handed down by our fathers, which were sacred, to fall into the hands of the Lamanites, (for the Lamanites would destroy them) therefore I made this record out of the plates of Nephi, and hid up in the hill Cumorah all the records which had been entrusted to me by the hand of the Lord, save it were these few plates which I gave unto my son Moroni.

The third was to complete the abridgement of the records, which would become the bulk of *The Book of Mormon*. Included in this is the likely need to acquire the precious metal and to make plates.

Another goal was to preserve his son Moroni, so that Moroni could accomplish his primary commission—which we will discuss shortly.

Next he would need to acquire the material needed for Moroni's primary commission.

And also—and not insignificantly placed last on this list—he would attempt to preserve his people, if possible.

If Mormon needed only to save the records, and if he had enough gold to finish *The Book of Mormon*, then he could have remained an idle witness in hiding. However, his course of action was to put himself—along with any records he carried—in harm's way in order to accomplish the work that the Lord had set forth.

It would seem that Mormon had thought to include the vision of the brother of Jared in its entirety in his abridgement/compilation of *The Book of Mormon*. He knew the impact that it had when the

In other words, even as they retreated, it is likely that Mormon was doing his part to create and preserve an enduring record as commanded. It would also seem likely that Mormon would employ the talents of master craftsmen to have the gold formed into the blank plates that Moroni would use. That the blank plates were formed and bound with the others when Moroni was given custody of them is important in understanding the placement of Moroni's several sections of writing, and a clue as to the order in which they were written.

Some have suggested that Mormon might have lived on for a while after the great and last battle of the Nephite nation, and therefore that Moroni may not have been alone for that long. Our matrix exposes details that would suggest otherwise: We know that Mormon was a man of God, with specific primary responsibilities given to him from God. It is evidenced above that Mormon became again a leader of war in order to fulfill specific commandments regarding the lasting records. As such, he had just led 210,000 of his people to their death. There is no evidence of Mormon faintheartedness, but in fact there is evidence to the contrary as his decisions appear founded on specific duties that the Lord had given him. Based on these assignments, because the other major decisions that we know that he made appear to correlate with these assignments, and on the facts that the Nephite nation had just been destroyed and he too had figured to die in the great battle (Mormon 6:1, 7-10), we can surmise that the next choice that he made was also to be in support of those original obligations. All of these details indicate that the choice that he and those last two dozen Nephites made on that fateful day was most likely to give their lives either in a diversion or assault in order to distract the superior Laminate army and thereby give Moroni—and the records he carried—the best possible circumstance to escape capture by the enemy. This was to the end that Moroni could continue to protect the record and to do the work of inscribing onto lasting plates the record of the vision of the brother of Jared. Thus a small force would sacrifice itself to achieve a more important objective, just like the Spartans who blocked the road against the Persians at the battle of Thermopylae.

It would seem then that Mormon returned to lead the Nephites for the additional gold needed then gave his life in order to do all he could to ensure that the commandments of the Lord would be fulfilled. Similarly, Joseph Smith would later be commanded to hide and protect the sacred plates—promised by the Lord, through the prophet Moroni that if he did all that was in his power, that they would be preserved.

> **Pearl of Great Price, Joseph Smith, 1:59-60**
>
> **59** At length the time arrived for obtaining the plates, the Urim and Thummim, and the breastplate. ...the same heavenly messenger delivered them up to me with this charge: that I should be responsible for them;... *if I would use all my endeavors to preserve them, until he, the messenger, should call for them, they should be protected.*
>
> **60** I soon found out the reason why I had received such strict charges to keep them safe... But by the wisdom of God, they remained safe in my hands....

Though *The Book of Mormon* mentions a few Nephites who had at least temporarily escaped the battle and fled to the south, and/or defected to the Laminates (Mormon 6:15), it is logical to assume that after those 24 souls with Mormon had accomplished a maneuver to preserve Moroni and allowed his escape, that everyone Moroni knew had passed away, and that he would have travelled some distance and time from the battle to ensure the safety of the record, as well as his own.

Then he began his translation of the great vision of the world that was given to the brother of Jared after he saw the finger and then body of the Savior. To accomplish this, Moroni would have in hand the original 24 plates containing this vision, or a copy of the engravings on those plates.

> **Ether 1:2**
>
> 2And I take mine account from the twenty and four plates which were found by the people of Limhi, which is called the Book of Ether.

Moroni would also have carried and have use of the Urim and Thummim—the very set that the brother of Jared had been given, and the very set that would accompany the plates to the translator in the 19th century.

> **Ether 3:23-24**
>
> 23 And behold, *these two stones* will I give unto thee, and ye shall seal them up also with the things which ye shall write.
>
> 24 For behold, the language which ye shall write I have confounded; wherefore I will cause in my own due time that these stones shall magnify to the eyes of men these things which ye shall write.

> *Doctrine and Covenants*: 17:1
>
> 1 Behold, I say unto you, that you must rely upon my word, which if you do with full purpose of heart, you shall have a view of the plates, and also of the breastplate, the sword

> of Laban, the Urim and Thummim, which were given to
> the brother of Jared upon the mount, when he talked with
> the Lord face to face,...

And most likely also a written copy of this same vision in the Nephite language that was published at the time that Christ taught and expounded it. This Nephite copy was also included in the main historical record of the people, what we know as the large plates of Nephi.

> **3 Nephi 26:3-7**
>
> **3** And he did expound all things, even from the beginning until the time that he should come in his glory—yea, even all things which should come upon the face of the earth, even until the elements should melt with fervent heat, and the earth should be wrapt together as a scroll, and the heavens and the earth should pass away;
>
> **4** And even unto the great and last day, when all people, and all kindreds, and all nations and tongues shall stand before God, to be judged of their works, whether they be good or whether they be evil—
>
> **5** If they be good, to the resurrection of everlasting life; and if they be evil, to the resurrection of damnation; being on a parallel, the one on the one hand and the other on the other hand, according to the mercy, and the justice, and the holiness which is in Christ, who was before the world began.
>
> **6** And now there cannot be written in this book even a hundredth part of the things which Jesus did truly teach unto the people;
>
> **7** But behold the plates of Nephi do contain the more part of the things which he taught the people.

And we can compare these words of Nephi with Moroni's cursory explanation of the vision of the brother of Jared as included in his abridgement of the history of the Jaredites:

> **Ether 3:18**
>
> 18 *And he ministered unto him even as he ministered unto the Nephites*; and all this, that this man might know that he was God, because of the many great works which the Lord had showed unto him.

A copy in Nephite is also likely because the Nephites were a literate people at the time of their divine visitation, while the majority of the people that Christ taught in Palestine were not. This is indicated in the way that Christ taught the same principles to the two peoples that we know as the Sermon on the Mount: Note the difference: *"It is said that..."* Verses *"It is written that..."*

> **Matthew 5:21, 27, 33, & 43**
>
> 21 *Ye have heard that it was said by them of old time,* Thou shalt not kill; and whosoever shall kill shall be in danger of the judgment:
>
> 27 *Ye have heard that it was said by them of old time,* Thou shalt not commit adultery:
>
> 33 Again, *ye have heard that it hath been said by them of old time,* Thou shalt not forswear thyself, but shalt perform unto the Lord thine oaths:
>
> 43 *Ye have heard that it hath been said,* Thou shalt love thy neighbor, and hate thine enemy...

As compared to the same Sermon as given to the Nephites

3 Nephi 12:21, 27, 33 & 43

21 *Ye have heard that it hath been said by them of old time, and it is also written before you,* that thou shalt not kill, and whosoever shall kill shall be in danger of the judgment of God;

27 Behold, *it is written by them of old time,* that thou shalt not commit adultery;

33 And again *it is written,* thou shalt not forswear thyself, but shalt perform unto the Lord thine oaths;

43 And behold *it is written* also, that thou shalt love thy neighbor and hate thine enemy...

Thus Moroni translated this record from the original through the Urim and Thummim and probably assisted by a Nephite-language copy of the same; and scribed it—unabridged—onto golden plates, which plates were included as (at least part of, and one should suppose at least the lion share of) the sealed portion of the golden plates, which portion Joseph Smith was specifically charged to not translate.

This was the primary commission of Moroni. And we are not ready to have access to it.

2 Nephi 27: 10, 21

10 But the words which are sealed he shall not deliver, neither shall he deliver the book. For the book shall be sealed by the power of God, and the revelation which was sealed shall be kept in the book until the own due time of the Lord, that they may come forth; for behold, they reveal all things from the foundation of the world unto the end thereof.

21 Touch not the things which are sealed, for I will bring them forth in mine own due time; for I will show unto the children of men that I am able to do mine own work.

But when we are ready, the Lord has promised us—using the strongest language possible for us to understand—in His Own Name, that he will give it to us.

Ether 4:6-7

6 For the Lord said unto me: They shall not go forth unto the Gentiles until the day that they shall repent of their iniquity, and become clean before the Lord.

7 And in that day that they shall exercise faith in me, saith the Lord, even as the brother of Jared did, that they may become sanctified in me, then will I manifest unto them the things which the brother of Jared saw, even to the unfolding unto them all my revelations, saith Jesus Christ, the Son of God, the Father of the heavens and of the earth, and all things that in them are.

Undoubtedly then, this will come forth at a day when mankind is prepared to receive it, and with good reason is currently not made public.

In comparing the words of the vision to the words of *The Book of Mormon*, Moroni prayed:

Ether 12: 23-25, 27, 29

23 And I said unto him: Lord, the Gentiles will mock at these things, because of our weakness in writing; for Lord thou hast made us mighty in word by faith, but thou hast not made us mighty in writing; for thou hast made all this people that they could speak much, because of the Holy Ghost which thou hast given them;

24 And thou hast made us that we could write but little, because of the awkwardness of our hands. Behold, thou hast not made us mighty in writing like unto the brother of Jared, for thou madest him that the things which he wrote were mighty even as thou art, unto the overpowering of man to read them.

25 Thou hast also made our words powerful and great, even that we cannot write them; wherefore, when we write we behold our weakness, and stumble because of the placing of our words; and I fear lest the Gentiles shall mock at our words...

27... I give unto men weakness that they may be humble; and my grace is sufficient for all men that humble themselves before me; for if they humble themselves before me, and have faith in me, then will I make weak things become strong unto them.

29And I, Moroni, having heard these words, was comforted, and said: O Lord, thy righteous will be done, for I know that thou workest unto the children of men according to their faith;

We can be assured that when it is made public it will be powerful. As it quelled the virus of evil for generations of Nephites, so we can expect that it will inoculate the world for a thousand years.

2 Nephi 27:11

11 And the day cometh that the words of the book which were sealed shall be read upon the house tops; and they shall be read by the power of Christ; and all things shall

be revealed unto the children of men which ever have been among the children of men, and which ever will be even unto the end of the earth.

2 Nephi 30:15-18

15...for the earth shall be full of the knowledge of the Lord as the waters cover the sea.

16 Wherefore, the things of all nations shall be made known; yea, all things shall be made known unto the children of men.

17 There is nothing which is secret save it shall be revealed; there is no work of darkness save it shall be made manifest in the light; and there is nothing which is sealed upon the earth save it shall be loosed.

18 Wherefore, all things which have been revealed unto the children of men shall at that day be revealed; and Satan shall have power over the hearts of the children of men no more, for a long time...

The words of the Lord to Moroni suggest an exception:

Ether 4:7

6 For the Lord said unto me: They shall not go forth unto the Gentiles until the day that they shall repent of their iniquity, and become clean before the Lord.

7 And in that day that they shall exercise faith in me, saith the Lord, even as the brother of Jared did, that they may become sanctified in me, then will I manifest unto them the things which the brother of Jared saw...

This, and the words of Alma to Zeezrom:

Alma 12:9

9 And now Alma began to expound these things unto him, saying: It is given unto many to know the mysteries of God; nevertheless they are laid under a strict command that they shall not impart only according to the portion of his word which he doth grant unto the children of men, according to the heed and diligence which they give unto him.

—demonstrate that the timeline of this promise may also extend prior to the millennium for individuals who are prepared as described, and to whom, therefore, such a vision will not inhibit agency.

In summation: Moroni had the 24 plates of the Jaredites, the Urim and Thummim set that the brother of Jared had been given by the Lord, (most likely) a copy of this same record in the Nephite language (see Ether 12:25), training from his Father and the divine commission to do so. He completed the unabridged, word for word transcription of the great vision of the brother of Jared onto golden plates that were compiled with *The Book of Mormon*, and he translated by the power of revelation through the seer-stones. Orson Pratt reported that the sealed portion was about two-thirds of the total. (New Era Magazine, Church of Jesus Christ of Latter-day Saints, July 2007 "What did the Golden Plates Look Like?") And if we surmise that it the bulk of the sealed portion of the plates is the unabridged vison of the brother of Jared, then this indicates that Moroni wrote on about twice as many plates as did his father. This had to have been an amazing experience for Moroni.

Next, he abridged the general record of the Jaredites. This is the Book of Ether, with Moroni's editorial statements included in Ether 2:9-12, 3:17-28, and chapters 4, 5, and 12. This chronological order is indicated by his mentioning the preceding work in Ether 3,—that the brother of Jared received the great vision; Ether 4,—that Moroni was charged to transcribe it onto the plates; and Ether 12 wherein Moroni again cuts into the history with a lesson about why there are fundamental differences between the strength of these words and the words of the of the brother of Jared in describing the great vision.

Next, somewhere around about this time, or perhaps simultaneously with the writing of the balance of the book of Moroni, this prophet began the work on the end-notes section of his writings. His exhortations had a different scope as compared to the "intent" that his father had tagged to the end of his part of the record in Mormon 7, or of the "intent" of Nephi (1), as found in 2 Nephi 31-32. Moroni's would become what we now know as Moroni 10: 3-30. It appears to that the first two verses (the time-stamp) and the last few verses (the softened re-direct) were added either when it was actually scribed into the gold, or that spaces were set aside on the plates for those verses.

After all that Moroni had seen, heard, lived through and translated, his closing statements were a list of eight exhortations, each one a lesson in itself. The list was initiated prior to some of his other engravings, apparently on space on the plates reserved for their inclusion, as indicated by his later comment located just after the record of his father.

> **Mormon 8:5-6**
>
> 5 Behold, my father hath made this record, and he hath written the intent thereof. And behold, I would write it also if I had room upon the plates, but I have not; and ore I have none, for I am alone...
>
> 6 Behold, four hundred years have passed away since the coming of our Lord and Savior.

Moroni mentions that Mormon had written the intent, which we know as Mormon 7, which is 10 verses—a mere 463 words—yet Moroni said that he did not have the space to repeat the concepts as a second testifier, but instead simply refers us back to it. In this he announces that he had already used most of the space on the plates and indicates that he had already allocated any heretofore unused space on the plates for specific work.

Upon the completion of his primary commission, and secondarily of the abridgement of the Jaredite record, it is important to note that Moroni had thought that he would not write anything more.

> **Moroni 1:1**
>
> 1Now I, Moroni, after having made an end of abridging the account of the people of Jared, I had supposed not to have written more,..

And

> **Ether 12:38-41**
>
> 38 And now I, Moroni, bid farewell unto the Gentiles, yea, and also unto my brethren whom I love, until we shall meet before the judgement-seat of Christ, where all men shall know that my garments are not spotted with your blood.
>
> 39 And then shall ye know that I have seen Jesus, and that he hath talked with me face to face, and that he told me in plain humility, even as a man telleth another in mine own language, concerning these things;
>
> 40 And only a few have I written, because of my weakness in writing.
>
> 41 And now, I would commend you to seek this Jesus of whom the prophets and apostles have written, that the

grace of God the Father, and also the Lord Jesus Christ, and the Holy Ghost, which beareth record of them, may be and abide in you forever. Amen.

—where he bids farewell, shares his apostolic testimony, and commends the reader to seek this Jesus. Later, in Moroni 10, his eight exhortations actually outline some important ways to do just that. This implies that the transcription of the great vision and the abridgment of the Jaredite record had the highest priority in the use of the lasting plates, and therefore also of Moroni's time.

Fourth, Moroni wrote the book of Moroni, or at least the first nine chapters of it. Chapters 7-9 were copied from letters that he carried from his father. This also suggests that Moroni, in his years of loneliness, carried other letters from his father as well, perhaps letters that did not make the cut to be scribed onto gold plates, but one can imagine that they were words of wisdom and encouragement from a loving father who had been given to know that Moroni would be alone.

Fifth, he wrote the part we know as Mormon chapters 8 and 9. Perhaps he filled in the balance of the last plate that Mormon had scribed upon. There are indicators that Mormon 8 and 9 were written after Moroni 9, including that Moroni did not include the letters from his father as part of his father's record and that he indicates that he had minimal space left on the plates and no ore to make additional plates (Mormon 8:5).

Mormon 8-9 include a series of warnings/strong counsel to all who have the opportunity to receive this record, which is similar to the way that Nephi (1) ended his writings.

2 Nephi 33:10-11

10 And now, my beloved brethren, and also Jew, and all ye ends of the earth, hearken unto these words and believe in Christ; and if ye believe not in these words believe in Christ...

11 And if they are not the words of Christ, judge ye—for Christ will show unto you, with power and great glory, that they are his words, at the last day; and you and I shall stand face to face before his bar; and ye shall know that I have been commanded of him to write these things...

As compared with Moroni's words in at the end of his father's record:

Mormon 8:16-17, 21 (See also verses 18-19)

16 And blessed be he that shall bring this thing to light... and it shall be done by the power of God.

17 ...therefore, he that condemneth, let him be aware lest he shall be in danger of hell fire.

18 And he that saith: Show unto me, or ye shall be smitten—let him beware lest he commandeth that which is forbidden of the Lord.

21And he that shall breathe out wrath and strifes against the work of the Lord... and shall say: We will destroy the work of the Lord, and the Lord will not remember his covenant which he hath made unto the house of Israel—the same is in danger to be hewn down and cast into the fire;

Another signal that these two chapters are written after Ether 12 is because Moroni demonstrates that he learns an important lesson about words of *The Book of Mormon* vs. the words of the great vision of the brother of Jared, and then Mormon 8:12 refers to that lesson, in a caution that it might not be a stumbling block for the student of this record.

First the lesson:

Ether 12: 23-29

23 And I said unto him: Lord, the Gentiles will mock at these things, because of our weakness in writing; for Lord thou hast made us mighty in word by faith, but thou hast not made us mighty in writing; for thou hast made all this people that they could speak much, because of the Holy Ghost which thou hast given them;

24 And thou hast made us that we could write but little, because of the awkwardness of our hands. Behold, thou hast not made us mighty in writing like unto the brother of Jared, for thou madest him that the things which he wrote were mighty even as thou art, unto the overpowering of man to read them.

25 Thou hast also made our words powerful and great, even that we cannot write them; wherefore, when we write we behold our weakness, and stumble because of the placing of our words; and I fear lest the Gentiles shall mock at our words.

26 And when I had said this, the Lord spake unto me, saying: Fools mock, but they shall mourn; and my grace is sufficient for the meek, that they shall take no advantage of your weakness;

27 And if men come unto me I will show unto them their weakness. I give unto men weakness that they may be humble; and my grace is sufficient for all men that humble

themselves before me; for if they humble themselves before me, and have faith in me, then will I make weak things become strong unto them.

28 Behold, I will show unto the Gentiles their weakness, and I will show unto them that faith, hope and charity bringeth unto me—the fountain of all righteousness.

29 And I, Moroni, having heard these words, was comforted, and said: O Lord, thy righteous will be done, for I know that thou workest unto the children of men according to their faith;

Then, in referring to the lesson:

Mormon 8:12

12 And whoso receiveth this record, and shall not condemn it because of the imperfections which are in it, the same shall know of greater things than these...

There will be more discussion on this point in the chapter entitled "Nephi's Theme."

Also compare

Mormon 9:30-31 (See also verses 32-33)

30 Behold, I speak unto you as though I spake from the dead; for I know that ye shall have my words.

31 Condemn me not because of mine imperfection, neither my father, because of his imperfection, neither them who have written before him; but rather give thanks unto God that he hath made manifest unto you our imperfections, that ye may learn to be more wise than we have been.

Between Mormon chapter 7 and Mormon chapter 8, Sixteen years had gone by since Mormon died.

> **Mormon 6:5**
>
> 5 And when three hundred and eighty and four years had passed away, we had gathered in all the remainder of our people unto the land of Cumorah.
>
> **Mormon 8:6**
>
> 6 Behold, four hundred years have passed away since the coming of our Lord and Savior.

From what is known of Moroni, it is—of course—inconceivable that he would have wasted that time.

As previously mentioned, it appears that the exhortations that comprise the body of chapter 10 of the Book of Moroni, were already planned and space on the plates allocated for this final chapter years before the work was completed, perhaps even scribed into the plates in the 16-year period prior to the writing of Mormon chapters 8 and 9. Be that as it may, it would seem that there were a couple of verses added at the beginning of this section and a few added at the end, when he was a much older man:

The first and most obvious are the first two verses of this section of his work:

> **Moroni 10:1-2**
>
> 1 Now I, Moroni, write somewhat as seemeth me good; and I write unto my brethren, the Lamanites; and I would that they should know that more than four hundred years have passed away since the sign was given of the coming of Christ.

2 And I seal up these records, after I have spoken a few words by way of exhortation unto you.

These two verses are an intentional time-stamp indicating the date that the record was sealed up. It also serves as a short introduction to the list of exhortations.

The next two segments that were added are less obvious. In both cases they point to a man, a prophet of God, a prophet who was privileged to see the vision of the brother of Jared, who continued to change, to improve before the Lord. After the last exhortation, Moroni elected to include some endnotes as he finished the record. He expounded upon his last exhortation, which reads:

Moroni 10: 30

30 And again I would exhort you that ye would come unto Christ, and lay hold upon every good gift, and touch not the evil gift, nor the unclean thing.

Here Moroni is reminding the reader that he had had access to the vision of the brother of Jared, that he had seen our day and knew that many would have a problem with believing that God could still do miracles. (See Mormon 9:15-37.) This record was a miraculous gift: Its creation was a miracle, its translation would be a miracle, and mankind would need to accept miracles to accept this record.

And what was said and might have been considered complete in one verse was then expanded to four:

Moroni 10:31-33

31 And awake, and arise from the dust, O Jerusalem; yea, and put on thy beautiful garments, O daughter of Zion; and strengthen thy stakes and enlarge thy borders forever, that thou mayest no more be confounded, that the covenants of the Eternal Father which he hath made unto thee, O house of Israel, may be fulfilled.

32 Yea, come unto Christ, and be perfected in him, and deny yourselves of all ungodliness; and if ye shall deny yourselves of all ungodliness, and love God with all your might, mind and strength, then is his grace sufficient for you, that by his grace ye may be perfect in Christ; and if by the grace of God ye are perfect in Christ, ye can in nowise deny the power of God.

33 And again, if ye by the grace of God are perfect in Christ, and deny not his power, then are ye sanctified in Christ by the grace of God, through the shedding of the blood of Christ, which is in the covenant of the Father unto the remission of your sins, that ye become holy, without spot.

This is the more positive voice of Moroni, explaining to us to do more than just stay out of the mud because it is dirty. He describes the blessings that await us, and the miracle in which we may be made clean.

As you might expect, the last verse was also added later also. Again, though he had seen our day, there is another marker that the last few verses were added later, and as postulated much later than the main body of the exhortations of Moroni in chapter 10. It is possible that the very last verse was added later, because 1) it is a farewell note, as it indicates that he is feeling old. And 2)—like verse 27—it refers to meeting at the judgement bar of God, but this time instead of a warning, it's a more positive note.

> **Moroni 10:27**
>
> **27** And I exhort you to remember these things; for the time speedily cometh that ye shall know that I lie not, for ye shall see me at *the bar of God*; and the Lord God will say unto you: Did I not declare my words unto you, which were written by this man, like as one crying from the dead, yea, even as one speaking out of the dust?

Compare with:

> **Moroni 10:34**
>
> **34** And now I bid unto all, farewell. I soon go to rest in the paradise of God, until my spirit and body shall again reunite, and I am brought forth triumphant through the air, to meet you before *the pleasing bar of the great Jehovah*, the Eternal Judge of both quick and dead. Amen.

Decades of loneliness had passed, and Moroni was a changed man. And whereas the sternness of the warning may have directed those who were not in the path to step up, I'm sure that in this restatement, his words appeal to and inspire those who are in the path and looking forward.

In a subsequent chapter we will discuss a series of logical steps based on the details of the record that indicate that Moroni probably started by engraving Mormon 6 as dictated by his father,—after Mormon 7.

Most of Moroni's engraving work was accomplished prior to the time-stamp in Mormon 8, and—along with the strong likelihood that Mormon and the other 24 who survived the climactic day of the last great Nephite battle gave their lives to help ensure Moroni's escape—indicates that Moroni spent a long time on his own, securing nearly completed plates before their final disposition at Cumorah.

++++

One matrix meshes with another, adding dimension. Having set the chronological order of the writings of Moroni, we return to the specifics leading up to the lesson that he learned while translating, transcribing, and abridging the writings of the brother of Jared.

Moroni had learned that the brother of Jared has seen the finger of the Lord, then body of the Lord.

> **Ether 3:9-13**
>
> **9** And the Lord said unto him: Because of thy faith thou hast seen that I shall take upon me flesh and blood; and never has man come before me with such exceeding faith as thou hast; for were it not so ye could not have seen my finger. Sawest thou more than this?
>
> **10** And he answered: Nay; Lord, show thyself unto me.
>
> **11** And the Lord said unto him: Believest thou the words which I shall speak?
>
> **12** And he answered: Yea, Lord, I know that thou speakest the truth, for thou art a God of truth, and canst not lie.
>
> **13** And when he had said these words, behold, the Lord showed himself unto him,

He then was permitted to see a "great many works".

Ether 3:17-28

17 And now, as I, Moroni, said I could not make a full account of these things which are written, therefore it sufficeth me to say that Jesus showed himself unto this man in the spirit, even after the manner and in the likeness of the same body even as he showed himself unto the Nephites.

18 And he ministered unto him even as he ministered unto the Nephites; and all this, that this man might know that he was God, because of the many great works which the Lord had showed unto him.

Moroni mentions that the Lord "ministered unto him even as he ministered unto the Nephites". Obviously not in that chronological order, but most likely in the order in which Moroni had learned of these events. The important side-note here is that both the brother of Jared and the Nephites living at ~34 A.D. were ministered to personally by the Lord, and taught of his great many works.

He was then commissioned by the Lord to write the things that he was about to see, but to keep this record from the people.

Ether 3:21-28

21 And it came to pass that the Lord said unto the brother of Jared: Behold, thou shalt not suffer these things which ye have seen and heard to go forth unto the world, until the time cometh that I shall glorify my name in the flesh; wherefore, ye shall treasure up the things which ye have seen and heard, and show it to no man.

22 And behold, when ye shall come unto me, ye shall write them and shall seal them up, that no one can interpret them; for ye shall write them in a language that they cannot be read.

23 And behold, these two stones will I give unto thee, and ye shall seal them up also with the things which ye shall write.

24 For behold, the language which ye shall write I have confounded; wherefore I will cause in my own due time that these stones shall magnify to the eyes of men these things which ye shall write.

25 And when the Lord had said these words, he showed unto the brother of Jared all the inhabitants of the earth which had been, and also all that would be; and he withheld them not from his sight, even unto the ends of the earth.

26 For he had said unto him in times before, that if he would believe in him that he could show unto him all things—it should be shown unto him; therefore the Lord could not withhold anything from him, for he knew that the Lord could show him all things.

27 And the Lord said unto him: Write these things and seal them up; and I will show them in mine own due time unto the children of men.

28 And it came to pass that the Lord commanded him that he should seal up the two stones which he had received, and show them not, until the Lord should show them unto the children of men.

Apparently, with the exception of the brother of Jared, the Jaredites were not ready at that time to receive that knowledge.

When the record was found by the people of Limhi and translated by King Mosiah(2) the Nephites at that time were apparently not ready to receive it either. For even though King Mosiah was a seer (Mosiah 8:13-14) and therefore able to translate ancient records, and though there was an opportunity to include the reading of this record along with the historical record of the people of Zeniff and of the people of Alma, there is no mention of that sacred text being shared at that time. (Mosiah 25:4-7)

However, there was some hint about it as one prophet handed off custodianship to the next:

Alma 37:2, 11-14

2...and keep all these things sacred which I have kept, even as I have kept them; for it is for a wise purpose that they are kept.

11 Now these mysteries are not yet fully made known unto me; therefore I shall forbear.

12 And it may suffice if I only say they are preserved for a wise purpose, which purpose is known unto God; for he doth counsel in wisdom over all his works, and his paths are straight, and his course is one eternal round.

13 O remember, remember, my son Helaman, how strict are the commandments of God. And he said: If ye will keep my commandments ye shall prosper in the land—but if ye keep not his commandments ye shall be cut off from his presence.

14 And now remember, my son, that God has entrusted you with these things, which are sacred, which he has kept sacred, and also which he will keep and preserve for a wise purpose in him, that he may show forth his power unto future generations.

So, according to the recorded will of God in the matter, the vision was kept from the people, most likely so that the unprepared would not be responsible for having that information, and that it did not impinge on personal agency. Instead, it was kept from the people and passed from prophet to prophet.

> **Ether 3:27-28**
>
> **27** And the Lord said unto him: Write these things and seal them up; and I will show them in mine own due time unto the children of men.
>
> **28**And it came to pass that the Lord commanded him that he should seal up the two stones which he had received, and show them not, until the Lord should show them unto the children of men.

And so it was protected (or the people protected from it) throughout the generations until—after the destruction of the more wicked part of the people—Christ showed himself to the Nephites at Bountiful. Then and per plan, the Lord shared with them the vision of the brother of Jared to the Nephites. I refer again to those verses:

> **Ether 3:17-18**
>
> **17** And now, as I, Moroni, said I could not make a full account of these things which are written, therefore it sufficeth me to say that Jesus showed himself unto this man in the spirit, even after the manner and in the like-ness of the same body even as he showed himself unto the Nephites.
>
> **18** And he ministered unto him even as he ministered unto the Nephites; and all this, that this man might know that he was God, because of the many great works which the Lord had showed unto him.

These verses describe that the parallelism of experience of the Nephites and of the brother of Jared was more than just seeing the body of Jesus Christ, but also indicates that the Nephites were ministered unto even as was the brother of Jared, to the end that they would know that the Lord was God, because of the many great works the Lord had showed unto them: They received the information that the brother of Jared had received in a vision 2000 years before.

Further, it is possible and likely that this knowledge that was shared with the people when Jesus Christ "expound(ed) all things unto them" was a substantial part of the inoculation of four generations from the temptations of the adversary. We should expect that when the Savior comes, that this same record that Moroni has transcribed and is currently sealed from our view, will be a significant part of the knowledge of God that will spread across the world.

According to Mormon's explanation near the end of the record of Christ's visit to the Nephites, the bulk of what the Lord shared with the Nephites and the brother of Jared prior to them was not to be included in *The Book of Mormon* for all to have at this time:

> **3 Nephi 26: 6-8**
>
> **6** And now there cannot be written in this book even a hundredth part of the things which Jesus did truly teach unto the people;
>
> **7** But behold the plates of Nephi do contain the more part of the things which he taught the people.
>
> **8** And these things have I written, which are a lesser part of the things which he taught the people; and I have written them to the intent that they may be brought again unto this people, from the Gentiles, according to the words which Jesus hath spoken.

> 9 And when they shall have received this, which is expedient that they should have first, to try their faith, and if it shall so be that they shall believe these things then shall the greater things be made manifest unto them.
>
> 10 And if it so be that they will not believe these things, then shall the greater things be withheld from them, unto their condemnation.
>
> 11 Behold, I was about to write them, all which were engraven upon the plates of Nephi, but the Lord forbade it, saying: I will try the faith of my people.

The Jaredites were the Lord's people, and were given great blessings including a promised land, but they were not permitted the knowledge of this vision. The Nephites were the Lord's people, and were not permitted to have this knowledge until the Savior presented it to the remaining, more-righteous part of the people in 34 A.D. And we know that though Mormon had thought to do so, the Lord forbade him from including this information in *The Book of Mormon.* So at least in our current general ignorance of this special content, we are in good company.

Moroni would have included the information also: Keep in mind that Moroni wrote Mormon 8 and 9 after he had completed the work that is in the sealed portion. His promise to us is significant:

> **Mormon 8:12**
>
> 12 And whoso receiveth this record, and shall not condemn it because of the imperfections which are in it, the same shall know of greater things than these. Behold, I am Moroni; and were it possible, I would make all things known unto you.

This is *almost* an oath, the significance of which should not be overlooked: Remember that once upon a time, oaths had been a common thing among the Nephites: Nephi and Zoram made oaths to one another, resulting in Zoram being saved from the destruction that would befall Jerusalem (1 Nephi 4:31-37.) The same Nephi had used an oath to guide and guarantee that he and his brothers would acquire the brass plates (1 Nephi 3:15) and soon after Laman and Lemuel decided to go clubbing—they beat Nephi with a rod—ostensibly because the oath that Nephi had made could be extinguished with his demise. (2 Nephi 3:28.) Later, Christ brought the higher law, and oaths of this nature—along with their potential trouble—were set aside. (3 Nephi 12:33-37) Oaths could sometimes be abused, and/or become more trouble than they were worth. This change in the use of oaths is similar to the Word of Wisdom wherein certain substances were no longer permitted to be taken into our bodies. *(Doctrine and Covenants 89:3)* Arguably, both were for the same reason: "…adapted to the capacity of the weak and weakest…"

So when Moroni speaks to the reader in

> **Mormon 8:12:**
>
> 12 … "Behold, I am Moroni…"

—he was not just introducing himself. He had already done so eleven verses earlier. (Mormon 8:1) In today's language Moroni wrote: "I swear, in the highest way that God will currently allow in this situation, that if it were possible, I would show you all things." The implication is clear: In this reading, we are only getting to see the tip of the iceberg of what exists. The vision of the brother of Jared included the entire history of the world. It was not possible for Moroni to include it in *The Book of Mormon* because God did not want it included, and Moroni knew it.

At this point, having learned the lesson covered in the middle of Ether chapter 12, Moroni understood that it was not his role, nor was it the role of his father to short-circuit the will of the Lord as described by Alma to Zeezrom nearly 500 years before:

> **Alma 12:9-10**
>
> 9 ...It is given unto many to know the mysteries of God; nevertheless they are laid under a strict command that they shall not impart only according to the portion of his word which he doth grant unto the children of men, according to the heed and diligence which they give unto him.
>
> 10 And therefore, he that will harden his heart, the same receiveth the lesser portion of the word; and he that will not harden his heart, to him is given the greater portion of the word, until it is given unto him to know the mysteries of God until he know them in full.

Moroni saw evidence of Alma's words in the Jaredite record:

> **Ether 12:5**
>
> 5 And it came to pass that Ether did prophesy great and marvelous things unto the people, which they did not believe, because they saw them not.

It is possible that the Moroni was not simply speaking to some future time and people as readers of *The Book of Mormon*, but that he may also mean that if something changes—that is to say if *we* change somehow—that it would indeed be possible for him to show us all things.

Moroni endeavored to specifically teach directly to the people who would receive this record in the last days. He knew his audience: His lesson would not be flowing with metaphors and symbolism, it would be succinct and perhaps a bit abrupt. This is the start of Moroni's lesson to us, a lesson that he learned through pondering and prayer, while continuing to accomplish the task that God had called him to.

He declared:

Ether 12:12

12 For if there be no faith among the children of men God can do no miracle among them; wherefore, he showed not himself until after their faith.

This correlates nicely with:

Amos 3:7

7 Surely the Lord God will do nothing, but he revealeth his secret unto his servants the prophets.

It appears that in order to not infringe upon our agency, God sets some serious limits on his performance of miracles except among those who have faith in him. Also, as previously illustrated in the life of the brother of Jared, God is willing to wait for even the most faithful to step up so that they can be blessed. (Ether 2:13-25, 3:1-28)

Ether 12:20-21, 30

20 And behold, we have seen in this record that one of these was the brother of Jared; for so great was his faith in God, that when God put forth his finger he could not

hide it from the sight of the brother of Jared, because of his word which he had spoken unto him, which word he had obtained by faith.

21 And after the brother of Jared had beheld the finger of the Lord, because of *the promise* which the brother of Jared had obtained by faith, the Lord could not withhold anything from his sight; wherefore he showed him all things, for he could no longer be kept without the veil.

The promise referred to is in

Ether 3:11-13

11 And the Lord said unto him: Believest thou the words which I shall speak?

12 And he answered: Yea, Lord, I know that thou speakest the truth, for thou art a God of truth, and canst not lie.

13 And when he had said these words, behold, the Lord showed himself unto him, and said: *Because thou knowest these things ye are redeemed from the fall;* therefore ye are brought back into my presence; therefore I show myself unto you.

His calling and election were made sure by the word of the Lord. The two verses previous to the promise demonstrate the two other conditions that the Lord set just before he saw the great vision: After he had the brother of Jared answer to himself in the affirmative (I would posit that God already knew) that he would believe all of the words that the Lord would say, then the Lord showed himself to the prophet.

It is worth noting that quite a few of the writers of *The Book of Mormon* include that same testimony, that personal witness of the

Savior Jesus Christ. In particular, Moroni stated that he had seen the Lord,

> **Ether 12:39**
>
> **39**: And the shall ye know that I (Moroni) have seen Jesus, and that he hath talked with me face to face, and that he told me in plain humility, even as a man telleth another in mine own language, concerning these things; ...

and that his calling and election were made sure .

> **Ether 12:37**
>
> **37**: And it came to pass that the Lord said unto me: If they have not charity, it mattereth not unto thee, thou hast been faithful; wherefore, thy garments shall be made clean. And because thou hast seen thy weakness, thou shalt be made strong, even unto the sitting down in the place which I have prepared in the mansions of my Father.

Moroni also wrote that he had seen our day:

> **Mormon 8:35**
>
> **35** Behold, I speak unto you as if ye were present, and yet ye are not. But behold, Jesus Christ hath shown you unto me, and I know your doing.

Preceding this verse, in nine verses, Moroni prophesies of the coarseness of the world when *The Book of Mormon* will be brought forth. Specifically, he prophesies that *The Book of Mormon* shall arrive at a time in the history of the world when there is a severe lack of the belief in modern miracles.

Mormon 8:26

26 And no one need say they shall not come, for they surely shall, for the Lord hath spoken it; for out of the earth shall they come, by the hand of the Lord, and none can stay it; and it shall come in a day when it shall be said that miracles are done away; and it shall come even as if one should speak from the dead.

These verses are more of an actual description than the prophesyings of many who preceded him, which prophecies often include a great deal of symbolism. (i.e. Zenos' allegory of the olive vineyard in Jacob 5, and Lehi's/Nephi's vision of the tree of life in 1 Nephi 8 and 10-15.)

Mormon 8: 27-35

27 And it shall come in a day when the blood of saints shall cry unto the Lord, because of secret combination and the works of darkness.

28 Yea, it shall come in a day when the power of God shall be denied, and churches become defiled and be lifted up in the pride of their hearts; yea, even in a day when leaders of churches and teachers shall rise in the pride of their hearts, even to the envying of them who belong to their churches.

29 Yea, it shall come in a day when there shall be heard of fires, and tempests, and vapors of smoke in foreign lands;

30 And there shall also be heard of wars, rumors of wars, and earthquakes in divers places.

31 Yea, it shall come in a day when there shall be great pollutions upon the face of the earth; there shall be murders, and robbing, and lying, and deceivings, and

whoredoms, and all manner of abominations; when there shall be many who will say, Do this, or do that, and it mattereth not, for the Lord will uphold such at the last day. But wo unto such, for they are in the gall of bitterness and in the bonds of iniquity.

32 Yea, it shall come in a day when there shall be churches built up that shall say: Come unto me, and for your money you shall be forgiven of your sins.

33 O ye wicked and perverse and stiffnecked people, why have ye built up churches unto yourselves to get gain? Why have ye transfigured the holy word of God, that ye might bring damnation upon your souls? Behold, look ye unto the revelations of God; for behold, the time cometh at that day when all these things must be fulfilled.

34 Behold, the Lord hath shown unto me great and marvelous things concerning that which must shortly come, at that day when these things shall come forth among you.

35 Behold, I speak unto you as if ye were present, and yet ye are not. But behold, Jesus Christ hath shown you unto me, and I know your doing.

(See also vs. 36-41)

Unlike the Zenos, Moroni does not mention the exchange of olive branches anywhere. This is plain and clear.

Through carefully discovering the associations of smaller details with those that are more well known, we can begin to get a picture of what Moroni, the man, the prophet, the abridger, the writer and the editor was like. We also note the association between his seeing Christ, his calling and election made sure, his experiencing the vision of the brother of Jared, and how he knew how to teach his audience of this dispensation. I'm not certain if it is because we are

the temple in Jerusalem suggests they were well aware of the law of Moses and particularly the history commemorated in the Passover: That on the night of the first Passover the destroying angel came and killed off the firstborn, passing over only those who were inside a marked home. (Exodus 12:12) Then we can consider how "sore afraid" these shepherds must have been to see an angel on this, the Passover night.

> **Luke 2:9**
>
> **9** And, lo, the angel of the Lord came upon them, and the glory of the Lord shone round about them: and they were *sore afraid.*

These shepherds had been assigned to be out of place for the Passover. Of all the holidays in which to get called into work, it had to be this one. The only night of the year when seeing an angel would cause such dread. How comforting must have been the angel's first words:

> **Luke 2:10**
>
> **10**And the angel said unto them, *Fear not....*

The most important job that shepherds do is to witness the birth of a firstborn lamb so that with their testimony a first-born male lamb without blemish would be of value as a sacrifice at the temple. The angel called them to go and do their job. This time, to bear witness of The Lamb of God, the real sacrifice. And the sign as designated by the angel was that they would find him in swaddled and in a manger—a hewn-stone open-top box—just like they would use to put a first-born lamb so as to protect him from blemish to remain fit for sacrifice.

> **Luke 2:11-12**
>
> **11** For unto you is born this day in the city of David a Saviour, which is Christ the Lord.
>
> **12** And this *shall be* a sign unto you; Ye shall find the babe wrapped in swaddling clothes, lying in a manger.

For the privilege, and understanding the importance of their contribution, they went "with haste".

> **Luke 2: 15-17**
>
> **15** And it came to pass, as the angels were gone away from them into heaven, the shepherds said one to another, Let us now go even unto Bethlehem, and see this thing which is come to pass, which the Lord hath made known unto us.
>
> **16** And they came with haste, and found Mary, and Joseph, and the babe lying in a manger.
>
> **17** And when they had seen it they made known abroad the saying which was told them concerning this child.

Shifting back into the Americas, if we will consider some of the words from the voice of Christ during the time of the mists of darkness right after the great destruction:

> **3 Nephi 9: 15, 17, 19**
>
> **15** Behold, I am Jesus Christ the Son of God..
>
> **17**... and in me is the law of Moses fulfilled.
>
> **19** And ye shall offer up unto me no more the shedding of blood; yea, your sacrifices and your burnt offerings shall be done away, for I will accept none of your sacrifices and your burnt offerings.

We include the time-stamp of the appearance of Jesus Christ to the Nephites:

> **3 Nephi 10:18-19**
>
> **18** And it came to pass that in the ending of the thirty and fourth year, behold, I will show unto you that the people of Nephi who were spared, and also those who had been called Lamanites, who had been spared, did have great favors shown unto them, and great blessings poured out upon their heads, insomuch that soon after the ascension of Christ into heaven he did truly manifest himself unto them—
>
> **19** Showing his body unto them, and ministering unto them;

We note that when Mormon the editor, says "in the ending of the…year," he means *the last day*. This is indicated by the history of Teancum killing King Amalickiah:

> **Alma 51: 34-37**
>
> **34** And it came to pass that Teancum stole privily into the tent of the king, And put a javelin to his heart; and he did cause the death of the king immediately that he did not awake his servants.
>
> **35** And he returned again privily to his own camp, and behold, his men were asleep, and he awoke them and told them all the things that he had done.
>
> **36** And he caused that his armies should stand in readiness, lest the Lamanites had awakened and should come upon them.

> **37** *And thus endeth the twenty and fifth year of the reign of the judges* over the people of Nephi; and thus endeth the days of Amalickiah.

And in the very next verse:

> **Alma 52:1**
>
> 1 *And now, it came to pass in the twenty and sixth year of the reign of the judges* over the people of Nephi, behold, when the Lamanites awoke on the first morning of the first month, behold, they found Amalickiah was dead in his own tent; and they also saw that Teancum was ready to give them battle on that day.

From this we can determine that the Nephites who had survived the destruction at the time of Jesus Christ's death had not been observing the festivals and rituals of the law of Moses—especially not the convention of animal sacrifice—for just about a year. And whereas most of the sacrifices of the law of Moses were done at the temple (Joseph and Mary even took the baby Jesus to the temple to offer two turtle doves in his behalf, Luke 2: 22-24), the practice had been to slaughter the animal of the Passover at home as part of a special meal. (Exodus 12:8-11) It should come as no surprise then,

> **3 Nephi 10:18**
>
> 18...in the ending of the thirty and fourth year...

—that when the Passover rolled around again, since the law of Moses was fulfilled,

> **3 Nephi 11:1**
>
> 1...that there were a great multitude gathered together, of the people of Nephi, round about the temple which was in the land Bountiful; and they were marveling and wondering one with another...

—that the Nephites were gathered at the Bountiful Temple just as we would today for a conference which—in their case—replaced the previous house-bound celebration.

Thus the application of items from the Nephite calendar enhances certain details about the birth of Christ. It also illustrates that although the righteous remnant of the Nephites understood that Christ would eventually appear in person, that there was a particular motivation that caused 2500 of the people to gather at the temple at the beginning of the year.

CHAPTER 11

Mormon's Back Cover

Not only was the "back cover" of Mormon written sometime prior to the completion of his work, we will discover evidence that asserts that it was written prior to the chapter that appears right before it, and that there was space allotted for that in-between chapter.

Understanding that *The Book of Mormon* was not originally written, nor originally published with—for one example—chapter-breaks, nevertheless, they seem to fit well in this instance. First we will shine the light on the back-cover itself:

Moroni writes:

> **Mormon 8:5**
>
> 5 Behold, my father hath made this record, and *he hath written the intent thereof.* And behold, I would write it also if I had room upon the plates, but I have not; and ore I have none, for I am alone.

The "intent" of the book, as recorded by Mormon, and that Moroni refers to, is the last chapter that is attributed to Mormon, namely Mormon 7. Though I note that I could probably make my point without including it in its entirety, it is a magnificent though relatively short challenge to the world by a prophet of God, calling us all to come unto Christ and take hold of the blessings that await us in doing so.

Mormon 7

1 And now, behold, I would speak somewhat unto the remnant of this people who are spared, if it so be that God may give unto them my words, that they may know of the things of their fathers; yea, I speak unto you, ye remnant of the house of Israel; and these are the words which I speak:

2 Know ye that ye are of the house of Israel.

3 Know ye that ye must come unto repentance, or ye cannot be saved.

4 Know ye that ye must lay down your weapons of war, and delight no more in the shedding of blood, and take them not again, save it be that God shall command you.

5 Know ye that ye must come to the knowledge of your fathers, and repent of all your sins and iniquities, and believe in Jesus Christ, that he is the Son of God, and that he was slain by the Jews, and by the power of the Father he hath risen again, whereby he hath gained the victory over the grave; and also in him is the sting of death swallowed up.

6 And he bringeth to pass the resurrection of the dead, whereby man must be raised to stand before his judgement-seat.

7 And he hath brought to pass the redemption of the world, whereby he that is found guiltless before him at the judgment day hath it given unto him to dwell in the presence of God in his kingdom, to sing ceaseless praises with the

There is a difference between a battalion of ten thousand "being led", and a battalion of ten thousand "being led from the midst." On that day, Moroni led his assigned ten thousand, while Mormon along with the others who were listed among the dead, each led their assigned ten thousand "from the midst".

There are several items, which when viewed together help us to ascertain the history that demonstrates that the original plan of Mormon was probably to have Moroni "finish the record of the destruction of my people, the Nephites," (Mormon 6:1) though a reprieve from death was granted to Mormon which gave him the rights or at least the ability to complete that work. The evidence shows that Mormon scribed his "intent"—Mormon chapter 7—prior to the final battle. It stands to reason that Mormon left space for a chapter 6, which would describe the end of the Nephite nation. Further affirmation of this is the nature of those verses of scripture: Mormon begins to list the captains who had fallen with their thousands, (Mormon 6:12-15) and then cut this list short perhaps to use the space instead to express his anguish at their passing and a reminder of what is in store for them (Mormon 6:16-22) It would appear that, leaving nothing to chance, Mormon past the plates, interpreters, etc., to Moroni before the last battle.

Mormon 6:6

6 ...I made this record out of the plates of Nephi, and hid up in the hill Cumorah all the records which had been entrusted to me by the hand of the Lord, save it were these few plates which I gave unto my son Moroni.

And having given them to Moroni for safer keeping than he could provide, it would seem logical that Mormon probably also traded his somewhat safer battle-position with that of his son. However, God saved Mormon that day: (With what we know of

Nephite battles, we could speculate that perhaps a few of his most trusted guards remained to stand beside him when he traded positions with his son, and when their general was wounded, protected him with their bodies.) Though wounded, he was retrieved from the carnage of the field. It stands to reason then that Mormon would have dictated chapter 6 to his son Moroni, who scribed his words of the genealogy of battle-death, and the final words of the prophet-general over bodies of his fallen people.

Little details left by the editors allow us to piece together some of the important moments in the life of Mormon. The picture that it creates shows us that he was a man of God, who lived and served God in the best way that he knew. It shows the God left him his agency to choose and to figure out how best to act, and showed us why he was so great a leader among men in his own day, and such an example in ours.

CHAPTER 12

Moroni's Back Cover

M oroni had his own back-cover to include. It too was "in the can" early, perhaps even already transferred to the last golden plate with appropriate spacing for time-stamp and end-notes—the few verses preceding and after it—before he scribed Mormon chapters 8 and 9.

Though the message is certainly applicable to all, the listed target audience of Mormon's "intent" was gone, and Moroni specified another group to pay particular attention to his parting instructions. He looked at the world before him and spoke to those remaining in it:

> **Moroni 10:1, 2**
>
> 1 Now I, Moroni, write somewhat as seemeth me good; and I write unto my brethren, the Lamanites...
>
> 2 And I seal up these records, after I have spoken a few words by way of exhortation unto you.

His corresponds with the beginning of the Book of Moroni when he says:

Moroni 1:4

4 ... but I write a few more things, that perhaps they may be of worth unto my brethren, the Lamanites, in some future day, according to the will of the Lord.

To the Lamanites, he offered poignant encouragement to step up to the blessings that God has for them, with a series of eight exhortations. And it appears that even their order is important. We note that the back cover is actually all of Moroni 10:3-30 and perhaps even verse 31, but have included these selected verses to emphasis the list of exhortations.

Moroni 10:2, 3, 4, 7, 8, 18, 19, 27 & 30

2 And I seal up these records, after I have spoken a few words by way of *exhortation* unto you.

3 Behold, *I would exhort you* that when ye shall read these things, if it be wisdom in God that ye should read them, that ye would remember how merciful the Lord hath been unto the children of men, from the creation of Adam even down until the time that ye shall receive these things, and ponder it in your hearts.

4 And when ye shall receive these things, *I would exhort* you that ye would ask God, the Eternal Father, in the name of Christ if these things are not true; and if ye shall ask with a sincere heart, with real intent, having faith in Christ, he will manifest the truth of it unto you, by the power of the Holy Ghost....

7 And ye may know that he is, by the power of the Holy Ghost; wherefore *I would exhort you* that ye deny not the power of God; for he worketh by power, according to the faith of the children of men, the same today and tomorrow, and forever.

8 And again, *I exhort you*, my brethren, that ye deny not the gifts of God, for they are many; and they come from the same God. And there are different ways that these gifts are administered; but it is the same God who worketh all in all; and they are given by the manifestations of the Spirit of God unto men, to profit them....

18 And *I would exhort you*, my beloved brethren, that ye remember that every good gift cometh of Christ.

19 And *I would exhort you*, my beloved brethren, that ye remember that he is the same yesterday, today, and forever, and that all these gifts of which I have spoken, which are spiritual, never will be done away, even as long as the world shall stand, only according to the unbelief of the children of men....

27 And *I exhort you* to remember these things; for the time speedily cometh that ye shall know that I lie not, for ye shall see me at the bar of God; and the Lord God will say unto you: Did I not declare my word unto you, which were written by this man, like as one crying from the dead, yea, even as one speaking out of the dust?...

30 And again *I would exhort you* that ye would come unto Christ, and lay hold upon every good gift, and touch not the evil gift, nor the unclean thing.

It is noteworthy that twice he exhorts the reader to remember God's merciful and consistent workings among the children of men, which the totality of the record of *The Book of Mormon* represents. (Moroni 10:3,19) Through this he teaches that the gifts of the spirit are available in our dispensation as they were before, if we will prepare our lives and our hearts to receive them. This exhortation of remembering is reminiscent of the instruction that Moroni gave us in the beginning of Ether 12, when he recalled many of the great miracles that had been gifted upon mankind through their faith, and how faith was a necessary factor in their occurrence. He also associated these events with the nature of the verbiage that he would be able to include in *The Book of Mormon* vs. the strength and decisive power of the words of the brother of Jared that would be included in the sealed portion. Just as it was important for Lehi and his family to have the scriptures with them (1 Nephi 5:21-22) in the last verses of *The Book of Mormon*, Moroni reminded us that this was written that we might remember.

From an editor's perspective, the brother of Jared's insight into the importance of the work of a prophet (and therefore all of us) to actively seek revelation, and with the understanding that the Lord has methods to bless us with revelation without giving us "unearned" knowledge which would reduce our agency, we begin again a study of Nephi's writings:

CHAPTER 13

Nephi's Theme

The key to understanding the reason for Nephi's copying in all of those chapters of the book of Isaiah is to understand the reason why he copied a couple of the visions of Lehi at the beginning of his text—which were revelations that were most likely already included in the (lost) book of Lehi.

I would encourage you to identify a few friends who have been members of The Church of Jesus Christ of Latter-day Saints for at least several decades, and ask them how many times that they have read *The Book of Mormon*. In addition to their other scripture study, it would not be too unusual to find out that they have read that particular tome cover-to-cover literally dozens of times, and spent myriad hours in its study. I fall into this large group of people. While you are at it, ask them why they have read that 500+ page book of scripture so many times. Their answers might give pause: There is more to it than obligatory scripture study at the behest of their church leaders.

There are some wonderful things in that book. For instance, if one were to read it and sincerely test the promise made by Moroni (Moroni 10:3-5), he would discover that the book is true, would learn more of God's dealings with his prophets and mankind (Amos 3:7), would come to know that the entity that is the custodian of these things is the only true religion,and that this knowledge is a sacred gift from God to him/her personally.

Particularly, I write to those who have read *The Book of Mormon* many times. It is safe to say that most of the people in this group have a testimony of the truthfulness of this volume. Most of them recognize Nephi as one of the great prophets. Most of them have favorite verses in his books. Most of them have personally gained great knowledge and understanding of doctrine that has and will help them spiritually as well as temporally through the study of these books.

And finally, most would give Nephi just a passing grade on his writing ability.

To be fair, the writing initially comes off as lumpy gravy: Sure there's good stuff in it, just do not look at it too closely.

Perhaps at first appraisal these two books at appear as a disjointed collection of anecdotes from the life of Nephi and from his father, connected chronologically and by what appears to be (so named by at least to one well-versed and well-meaning commentator who will herein remain anonymous) Nephi's self-affection.

Perhaps at first appraisal it may seem that Nephi had family problems with more than just Laman and Lemuel. He describes his brother, Sam, with little more than a name, and what he says about his mother begins as an unflattering commentary about how her faith in the revelations received by her husband the prophet, had faltered.

> **1 Nephi 5:2-3**
>
> 2 For she had supposed that we had perished in the wilderness; and she also had complained against my father, telling

> him that he was a visionary man; saying: Behold thou hast led us forth from the land of our inheritance, and my sons are no more, and we perish in the wilderness.
>
> **3** And after this manner of language had my mother complained against my father.

He even includes a reminiscence of how his father, Lehi, murmured at one point.

> **1 Nephi 16:20**
>
> **20** And it came to pass that Laman, and Lemuel and the sons of Ishmael did begin to murmur exceedingly, because of their sufferings and afflictions in the wilderness; and also my father began to murmur against the Lord his God; yea, and they were all exceedingly sorrowful, even that they did murmur against the Lord.

Perhaps at first appraisal, Nephi seems to describe himself as the hero of his own manuscript, which runs contrary to the idea of a prophet being a humble servant of God. For example:

> **1 Nephi16:21-23**
>
> **21** Now it came to pass that I, Nephi, having been afflicted with my brethren because of the loss of my bow, and their bows having lost their springs, it began to be exceedingly difficult, yea, insomuch that we could obtain no food.
>
> **22** And it came to pass that I, Nephi, did speak much unto my brethren, because they had hardened their hearts again, even unto complaining against the Lord their God.
>
> **23** And it came to pass that I, Nephi, did make out of wood a bow, and out of a straight stick, an arrow; wherefore, I

> did arm myself with a bow and an arrow, with a sling and with stones. And I said unto my father: Whither shall I go to obtain food?

Perhaps at first appraisal, the inclusions of hearsay like the complaint of Sariah to Lehi as mentioned above (1 Nephi 5:2-3) and the two visions of Lehi that Nephi lead with in the very first chapter of his work might lend you to believe that Nephi is a poor writer by today's standard.

Perhaps at first appraisal, the historical unevenness of Nephi's record appears disconcerting: For example, two hundred and twenty-five verses cover the vision of the Tree of Life, and resulting queries, which took place over just a few days. (Seven chapters: 1 Nephi 8, 10-15) This is immediately followed and contrasted by 1 Nephi 16 where a mere thirty-nine verses covers the sons of Lehi marrying the daughters of Ishmael—with Zoram marrying the eldest daughter, Lehi receiving the Liahona and he and his family discovering (the hard way) some of its more unique features, travelling for four days, murmuring for want of food, chastening from the Lord, Nephi breaking his bow, Nephi making a new bow and finding food, giving thanks, travelling again for many days, Ishmael dying followed by more murmuring, and followed by more chastening.

Perhaps you have wondered if Nephi got bored with the idea of writing and if that could be the reason he let Jacob take over for a while. Just when we are getting used to the voice of Nephi vs. Isaiah, a third writer is tossed into the mix. Have you wondered why this would occur, especially since soon after, Jacob would get his own named book on the small plates?

Perhaps it has at times become a test of will to read through the many copied chapters of Isaiah, when it seems at first glance that

> **1 Nephi 19:2**
>
> **2** And I knew not at the time when I made them that I should be commanded of the Lord to make these plates...

The small plates were finite in number from their origin: Nephi created a bound volume.

> **Jarom 1:2**
>
> **2** And as these plates are small ...wherefore, it must needs be that I write a little...

> **Omni 1:30**
>
> **30**...these plates are full....

Per Nephi's instruction, the small plates were kept by the prophets.

> **1 Nephi 19:4**
>
> **4**...And this have I done, and commanded my people what they should do after I was gone; and that these plates should be handed down from one generation to another, or from one prophet to another, until further commandments of the Lord.

This continued until they were filled and then were given to King Benjamin (1), whom the keeper of the record at that time acknowledged as a righteous leader and therefore a safe custodian. (Omni 1:25)

Most of Nephi's editorial declarations are found in 1 Nephi 1, 6, 19, 2 Nephi 4: 14-35 (referred to as the Psalm of Nephi), 2 Nephi 5, 11, 31:3 and 2 Nephi 33—esp. vs. 4.

> **2 Nephi 33:4**
>
> 4 And I know that the Lord God will consecrate my prayers for the gain of my people. And the words which I have written in weakness will be made strong unto them; for it persuadeth them to do good; it maketh known unto them of their fathers; and it speaketh of Jesus, and persuadeth them to believe in him, and to endure to the end, which is life eternal.

In his various declarations we discover what he decided to not focus on in this record, definitions of just what it is he wants to illustrate, and who he is writing to. Instead of comparing these declarations as a discrete corpus of text, we elect to investigate them in the order and placement in which they appear in the scripture, inasmuch as their location enhances the understanding of their meaning. Moreover, if we view these declarations and aside-explanations as the skeletal framework of the writing, we can then visualize a listing of specific occurrences in his life that were strategically selected for this record to flesh out one grand concept: Nephi's theme.

Another important point is that Nephi did not copy all of the record of Isaiah that was found in the brass plates. In fact it appears that he did not even include all of the "good" parts: We know, for example that people of Zeniff took at least a partial copy of the brass plates with them when they separated from the main body of the Nephites. This is illustrated by the occurrence involving the wicked priests of Noah, when then sought to cross up Abinadi. From their accusations, they must have been dismissive of him and his "doom and gloom", and so asked him about the meaning of four verses of Isaiah 52, which were decidedly upbeat:

> **Mosiah 12: 21-24**
>
> 21 How beautiful upon the mountains are the feet of him that bringeth good tidings; that publisheth peace; that bringeth good tidings of good; that publisheth salvation; that saith unto Zion, Thy God reigneth;
>
> 22 Thy watchmen shall lift up the voice; with the voice together shall they sing; for they shall see eye to eye when the Lord shall bring again Zion;
>
> 23 Break forth into joy; sing together ye waste places of Jerusalem; for the Lord hath comforted his people, he hath redeemed Jerusalem;
>
> 24 The Lord hath made bare his holy arm in the eyes of all the nations, and all the ends of the earth shall see the salvation of our God?

And Abinidi responded by schooling them with a recitation of the entire 53rd chapter of Isaiah,—a chapter which is decidedly Messianic in content.

That is good stuff. That is what *The Book of Mormon, Another Testament of Jesus Christ* is about: Testifying of Christ.

With this in mind, there is a question to consider: How did Nephi determine which parts of the writings of Isaiah to include in his record?

Nephi was an older man when he began the small plates. There are several evidence of this that will be a part of this discussion, and they begin in the very first verse. Everything up to around 2 Nephi 5:31 is written in retrospect.

2 Nephi 5:28-33

28 And thirty years had passed away from the time we left Jerusalem.

29 And I, Nephi, had kept the records upon my plates, which I had made, of my people thus far.

30 And it came to pass that the Lord God said unto me: Make other plates; and thou shalt engraven many things upon them which are good in my sight, for the profit of thy people.

31 Wherefore, I, Nephi, to be obedient to the commandments of the Lord, went and made these plates upon which I have engraven these things.

32 And I engraved that which is pleasing unto God. And if my people are pleased with the things of God they will be pleased with mine engravings which are upon these plates.

33 And if my people desire to know the more particular part of the history of my people they must search mine other plates.

In other words, and for example, the history of Nephi slaying Laban with his own sword was written by Nephi after he had used that very sword several times in the protection of his people.

Nephi wrote according to a predetermined theme. He introduces it in the first chapter and—apart from some declarations and brief connecting (historical) sections—he stays generally true to this theme. The balance of this chapter will provide multiple examples. It appears that he had the examples of his theme lined up ahead of time that would become from 1 Nephi 1 to at least 2 Nephi 3. His editorial statements sections also include references to this theme.

Additionally, we will cite examples in Jacob and Enos where Nephi's theme was followed. Thus, we will demonstrate that Nephi was editor in absentia of the balance of the small plates that bear his name.

And then, using our understanding of this theme as a tool this work will:

- Investigate many of the anecdotes included in this record and with each begin to derive its purpose in selection as part of his small plates and learn about this theme from each story.
- In doing so, we may discover the reason that certain things were not included or simply glossed over, like the construction of the temple which is covered in exactly one verse.

> **2 Nephi 5:28-33**
>
> 16 And I, Nephi, did build a temple; and I did construct it after the manner of the temple of Solomon save it were not built of so many precious things; for they were not to be found upon the land, wherefore, it could not be built like unto Solomon's temple. But the manner of the construction was like unto the temple of Solomon; and the workmanship thereof was exceedingly fine.

Surely there were revelations on and spiritual experiences about how the temple was constructed, but this information did not pass the litmus test of the theme.

- Suggest reasons why certain chapters of Isaiah were included in specific locations in his work, and why this sheds light on the revelation that Nephi received and wanted to share from them.
- Point out insight extended to the reader by this tool about the words of Isaiah that seem to fit the purposes of Nephi.

- Suggest the use of the small plates of Nephi as a primer to be used to further our understanding of the Lord's plan for his people in these latter days, his plan for us personally or individually, and to help us in our quest to receive light that is greater than merely meeting the needs of the lower echelons of Maslow's pyramid.

> **Heading of the First Book of Nephi:**
>
> An account of Lehi and his wife Sariah, and his four sons, being called, (beginning at the eldest) Laman, Lemuel, Sam, and Nephi. The Lord warns Lehi to depart out of the land of Jerusalem, because he prophesieth unto the people concerning their iniquity and they seek to destroy his life. He taketh three days' journey into the wilderness with his family. Nephi taketh his brethren and returneth to the land of Jerusalem after the record of the Jews. The account of their sufferings. They take the daughters of Ishmael to wife. They take their families and depart into the wilderness. Their sufferings and afflictions in the wilderness. The course of their travels. They come to the large waters. Nephi's brethren rebel against him. He confoundeth them, and buildeth a ship. They call the name of the place Bountiful. They cross the large waters into the promised land, and so forth. This is according to the account of Nephi; or in other words, I, Nephi, wrote this record.

As we take a look at this heading, it reads as if Lehi and his family go here, do this, are sent there and react like this, etc. It appears at first blush to be the very history that Nephi says that it is not. (1 Nephi 9:2) This has led some to thinking that as viewed as a history a) Nephi must have had problems in his immediate family because he doesn't mention them very much in the record, and that this record was not even passed to his children, but to his brother,

Jacob, and then to Jacob's son, Enos. And b) that Nephi starts out easy-going enough, but his confidence becomes a bit self-serving in his writings.

Why does Nephi not mention much about his family in the small plates even though the narratives usually include interaction with them?

At the time that Nephi and his people separated themselves from those who would be generally known in the record as the Lamanites, Nephi's immediate family was still a measurable percentage of the total. Simply: There just were not that many people yet. Also we know that the subsequent kings were called after the name of Nephi.

> **Jacob 1:10-11**
>
> **10** The people having loved Nephi exceedingly, he having been a great protector for them, having wielded the sword of Laban in their defense, and having labored in all his days for their welfare—
>
> **11** Wherefore, the people were desirous to retain in remembrance his name. And whoso should reign in his stead were called by the people, second Nephi, third Nephi, and so forth, according to the reigns of the kings; and thus they were called by the people, let them be of whatever name they would.

Therefore it is very likely that the kings were—or at least the line began at—direct lineage of Nephi, that they (the kings) held and added to the large plates of Nephi (which was their history) and that the immediate family of Nephi claimed a significant portion of the first part of that record.

Nephi specifically states that these small plates of Nephi are not the history of the people, but that the history of the people is contained in other plates.

> **1 Nephi 19:1-4**
>
> 1 And it came to pass that the Lord commanded me, wherefore I did make plates of ore that I might engraven upon them the record of my people. And upon the plates which I made I did engraven the record of my father, and also our journeyings in the wilderness, and the prophecies of my father; and also many of mine own prophecies have I engraven upon them.

So if it was not written to be simply history, why do we tend to read it as if it were?

Perhaps we default to this practice because the anecdotes occurred anciently and chronologically.

And if Nephi did not intend it to be a history, then what did he intend it to be?

We should start by understanding to whom this record was written.

> **1 Nephi 19:3-4**
>
> 3 And after I had made these plates by way of commandment, I, Nephi, received a commandment that the ministry and the prophecies, the more plain and precious parts of them, should be written upon these plates; and that the things which were written should be kept for the instruction of my people, who should possess the land, and also for other wise purposes, which purposes are known unto the Lord.

and their receiving whatever other message that had been superimposed by the same power.

It is like the finding the integral of a mathematical function. This should be the same process for us when we read the scriptures or, for example, when we listen to the words of our current prophet and apostles.

Nephi's testimonies: At the beginning and at the end.

1 Nephi 1:2-3

2 Yea, I make a record in the language of my father, which consists of the learning of the Jews and the language of the Egyptians.

3 *And I know that the record which I make is true*; and I make it with mine own hand; and I make it according to my knowledge.

Nephi testifies that his record is true, and made according to his knowledge. He would again testify of the work's authenticity in the strongest of terms in the last chapter of his work:

2 Nephi 33:10-11

10 And now, my beloved brethren, and also Jew, and all ye ends of the earth, hearken unto these words and believe in Christ; and if ye believe not in these words believe in Christ. And if ye shall believe in Christ ye will believe in these words, *for they are the words of Christ, and he hath given them unto me*; and they teach all men that they should do good.

11 And if they are not the words of Christ, judge ye—for *Christ will show unto you, with power and great glory, that they are his words*, at the last day; and you and I shall stand face to face before his bar; and ye shall know that I have been commanded of him to write these things, notwithstanding my weakness.

These book-end testimonies are of themselves, evidence of a pre-designed theme of the work.

++++

And so it begins.

1 Nephi 1:4-15

4 For it came to pass in the commencement of the first year of the reign of Zedekiah, king of Judah, (my father, Lehi, having dwelt at Jerusalem in all his days); and in that same year there came many prophets, prophesying unto the people that they must repent, or the great city Jerusalem must be destroyed.

5 Wherefore it came to pass that my father, Lehi, as he went forth prayed unto the Lord, yea, even with all his heart, in behalf of his people.

6 And it came to pass as he prayed unto the Lord, there came a pillar of fire and dwelt upon a rock before him; and he saw and heard much; and because of the things which he saw and heard he did quake and tremble exceedingly.

7 And it came to pass that he returned to his own house at Jerusalem; and he cast himself upon his bed, being overcome with the Spirit and the things which he had seen.

8 And being thus overcome with the Spirit, he was carried away in a vision, even that he saw the heavens open, and he

thought he saw God sitting upon his throne, surrounded with numberless concourses of angels in the attitude of singing and praising their God.

9 And it came to pass that he saw One descending out of the midst of heaven, and he beheld that his luster was above that of the sun at noon-day.

10 And he also saw twelve others following him, and their brightness did exceed that of the stars in the firmament.

11 And they came down and went forth upon the face of the earth; and the first came and stood before my father, and gave unto him a book, and bade him that he should read.

12 And it came to pass that as he read, he was filled with the Spirit of the Lord.

13 And he read, saying: Wo, wo, unto Jerusalem, for I have seen thine abominations! Yea, and many things did my father read concerning Jerusalem—that it should be destroyed, and the inhabitants thereof; many should perish by the sword, and many should be carried away captive into Babylon.

14 And it came to pass that when my father had read and seen many great and marvelous things, he did exclaim many things unto the Lord; such as: Great and marvelous are thy works, O Lord God Almighty! Thy throne is high in the heavens, and thy power, and goodness, and mercy are over all the inhabitants of the earth; and, because thou art merciful, thou wilt not suffer those who come unto thee that they shall perish!

15 And after this manner was the language of my father in the praising of his God; for his soul did rejoice, and his whole heart was filled, because of the things which he had seen, yea, which the Lord had shown unto him.

Why does Nephi include an incident that he did not witness (hear-say), and that was probably already included in the book of Lehi?

The middle several verses—the body of this chapter—is the *introductory example* of an instance when a prophet—in this case, Lehi—asks for and at first receives revelation in a more simplistic or symbolic way. He sees a pillar of fire, and hears much. Next, he ponders and prays further about the things that he has just received, thereby preparing himself for more, and that's when the larger revelation is received. When he had further prepared himself, in the second revelation he "… saw God sitting upon his throne." He was also then given specific instructions on what to testify to/against the people.

The need for this pondering and prayer, of mental and spiritual preparation was expressed by the Savior, concluding his first sermon to the Nephites:

> **3 Nephi 17:2-3**
>
> **2** I perceive that ye are weak, that ye cannot understand all my words which I am commanded of the Father to speak unto you at this time.
>
> **3** Therefore, go ye unto your homes, and ponder upon the things which I have said, and ask of the Father, in my name, that ye may understand, and prepare your minds for the morrow, and I come unto you again.

The Savior was calling on them to take some time to prepare their hearts and minds through pondering and prayer in order that they might receive the greater light that he was to present to them.

It is noteworthy, however, that the little children were—in fact—already prepared for angels to minister unto them. We should explore the reasons for that, and *how* they were prepared. While certainly the Savior did not love His older children any less, it would appear that the little children were more prepared for the blessings received. And, by blessing the little children in this way, the Lord was able to bless *all* of those who were there to witness it.

Lehi was shown much, including even a book and bade to read it. What confidence it must have stirred in Lehi, to go forth and preach to the people, having been given the precise script to use for that work.

> **1 Nephi 1:6**
>
> **6** And now I, Nephi, do not make a full account of the things which my father hath written, for he hath written many things which he saw in visions and in dreams; and he also hath written many things which he prophesied and spake unto his children, of which I shall not make a full account.

He states that he will not be quoting all of the visions, ministries, and prophesies of his Father. And yet there are specific instances of his father's history (and even his mother's) that he *does* include in this record. Like this particular example which introduces his theme. It is also of note that he later states that this record contains a subset of even his own ministries and prophecies.

> **1 Nephi 19:3**
>
> **3** And after I had made these plates by way of commandment, I, Nephi, received a commandment that the ministry and the prophecies, the more plain and precious parts of them, should be written upon these plates...

As mentioned, some of the omitted material may include the likely flood of revelations that must have been received by the prophet for the construction and use of a temple on the American continent. (2 Nephi 5:16)

> **1 Nephi 1:17**
>
> **17** But I shall make an account of my proceedings in my days. Behold, I make an abridgment of the record of my father, upon plates which I have made with mine own hands; wherefore, after I have abridged the record of my father then will I make an account of mine own life.

Again, this is not a simple history of the life of Nephi. It begins with specific occurrences in the life of his father, and then continues with specific occurrences in his own life.

> **1 Nephi 1:18-20**
>
> **18** Therefore, I would that ye should know, that after the Lord had shown so many marvelous things unto my father, Lehi, yea, concerning the destruction of Jerusalem, behold he went forth among the people, and began to prophesy and to declare unto them concerning the things which he had both seen and heard.
>
> **19** And it came to pass that the Jews did mock him because of the things which he testified of them; for he truly testified of their wickedness and their abominations; and he testified that the things which he saw and heard, and also the things which he read in the book, manifested plainly of the coming of a Messiah, and also the redemption of the world.
>
> **20** And when the Jews heard these things they were angry with him; yea, even as with the prophets of old, whom they had cast out, and stoned, and slain; and they also sought his life, that they might take it away…

Verses 18-20: Lehi boldly went forth among the people, saying the things that he was instructed of the Lord to say. And the people did not have the ears to hear it, so much so that they sought his life. Even so, he was no less a prophet of God.

> **1 Nephi 1:20**
>
> **20...** But behold, I, Nephi, will show unto you that the tender mercies of the Lord are over all those whom he hath chosen, because of their faith, to make them mighty even unto the power of deliverance.

Elder Bednar gave a definitive sermon in General Conference highlighting this verse:

> **Liahona, 2005/5, Church of Jesus Christ of Latter-Day Saints "The Tender Mercies of the Lord" by Elder David A. Bednar. © Intellectual Reserve Inc.**
>
> Some individuals who hear or read this message erroneously may discount or dismiss in their personal lives the availability of the tender mercies of the Lord, believing that "I certainly am not one who has been or ever will be chosen." We may falsely think that such blessings and gifts are reserved for other people who appear to be more righteous or who serve in visible Church callings. I testify that the tender mercies of the Lord are available to all of us and that the Redeemer of Israel is eager to bestow such gifts upon us.
>
> To be or to become chosen is not an exclusive status conferred upon us. Rather, you and I ultimately determine if we are chosen. Please now note the use of the word *chosen* in the following verses from the Doctrine and Covenants: "Behold, there are many called, but few are *chosen*. And why are they not *chosen?* "Because their hearts are set so

much upon the things of this world, and aspire to the honors of men" (Doctrine and Covenants 121:34-35; emphasis added)

Enoch was instructed by the Lord on this very point of doctrine. Please note the use of the word *choose* in these verses: "Behold these thy brethren; they are the workmanship of mine own hands, and I gave unto them their knowledge, in the day I created them; and in the Garden of Eden, gave I unto man his agency;

"And unto thy brethren have I said, and also given commandment, that they should love one another, and that they should *choose* me, their Father" (Moses 7:32-33; emphasis added).

As we learn in these scriptures, the fundamental purposes for the gift of agency were to love one another and to choose God. Thus we become God's chosen and invite His tender mercies as we use our agency to choose God.

Continuing from Elder Bednar's same conference address:

(Elder David A. Bednar, ibid.)

"What are the tender mercies of the Lord? ... Through personal study, observation, pondering, and prayer, I believe I have come to better understand that the Lord's tender mercies are the very personal and individualized blessings, strength, protection, assurances, guidance, loving-kindnesses, consolation, support, and spiritual gifts which we receive from and because of and through the Lord Jesus Christ. Truly, the Lord suits "his mercies according to the conditions of the children of men" (Doctrine and Covenants 46:15)"

Nephi makes a great effort to demonstrate the importance of the tender mercy of revelation: To know the will of God, so that we might repent and align ourselves to it.

> **(Elder David A. Bednar, ibid)**
>
> One of the most well-known and frequently cited passages of scripture is found in Moses 1:39. This verse clearly and concisely describes the work of the Eternal Father: "For behold, this is *my work* and my glory—to bring to pass the immortality and eternal life of man" (emphasis added). A companion scripture found in the Doctrine and Covenants describes with equal clarity and conciseness our primary work as the sons and daughters of the Eternal Father. Interestingly, this verse does not seem to be as well-known and is not quoted with great frequency. "Behold, this is *your work*, to keep my commandments, yea, with all your might, mind and strength" (Doctrine and Covenants 11:20; emphasis added)."

To the mind that is focused mostly on the temporal, tender mercies might appear as mere coincidences. To the spiritually minded, all tender mercies are also recognized as forms of revelation, in that we see the hand of a loving God in our lives. Each and all of these revelations can and should be taken as signposts that help to mark the path that we are to follow. For our own sake, and for those who follow after us, these should be journaled into remembrance, especially for those times when these extra signposts may seem farther apart.

I intend to show evidence that Nephi's overall and original purpose in the creation of and engraving of the small plates was to demonstrate a method in which the chosen can prepare themselves to receive the tender mercy of divine revelation which is necessary to make them "mighty, even unto the power of deliverance."

> **Doctrine and Covenants 8:3**
>
> 3 Now, Behold, this is the spirit of revelation: behold, this is the spirit by which Moses brought the children of Israel through the Red Sea on dry ground.
>
> **Moses 1:25**
>
> 25 ...Blessed art thou Moses, for I, the Almighty, have chosen thee, and thou shalt be made stronger than many waters; for they shall obey thy commands as if thou wert God.

In other words, the tender mercies of God were manifested to Moses in that he received revelation that he had been given power to command the waters and deliver the Israelites to the relative safety of the desert beyond. Furthermore, I am confident that the fact that the spirit of revelation was the spirit by which Moses brought the people across the Red Sea on dry ground was not lost upon the camp of Lehi, particularly due to their proximity to it.

We should remember that the method of deliverance is dependent on the prison holding the Lord's people. For example, at the blessing of John the Baptist:

> **Luke 1:67,76-79**
>
> 67 And his father Zacharias was filled with the Holy Ghost, and prophesied, saying...
>
> 76 And thou, child, shalt be called the prophet of the Highest: for thou shalt go before the face of the Lord to prepare his ways;
>
> 77 To give knowledge of salvation unto his people by the remission of their sins,

78 Through the tender mercy of our God; whereby the dayspring from on high hath visited us,

79 To give light to them that sit in darkness and in the shadow of death, to guide our feet into the way of peace.

In all cases, the Lord's tender mercies are to guide our feet into the way of peace, which means, to Him.

I hypothesis that the "tender mercies" spoken of in 1 Nephi 1:20 refer mostly to divine revelation.

I postulate that though God loves and wants to bless his children, except in a rare handful of occurrences—which if we had greater understanding we would probably discover are actually *not* exceptions to the rule*—He wants to bless us with spiritual knowledge without inhibiting our agency.(* For example, An angel visits Laman and Lemuel when they attempt to close the oath of action that Nephi had made by assisting him to forfeit his life. 1 Nephi 3:28-31)

The initial example of methodology as listed above is tabled as follows:

	The reception of the initial spiritual knowledge (and then personal preparation)	A greater divine revelation is received
1 Nephi 1	Lehi received the vision of the pillar of fire, and also heard things. (**1 Nephi 1:5-6**) Then Lehi took some time to ponder and pray about what he had received so far. (**1 Nephi 1:7**)	Lehi saw the heavens opened, saw God the Father and his Son, and learned that Jerusalem would be destroyed. (**1 Nephi 1:8-15**)

For clarity, I have continued the list in a table, with breaks for Nephi's editorial declarations.

1 Nephi 2

The reception of the initial spiritual knowledge, and then personal preparation:

Lehi (and therefore his family through him) received a revelation to leave Jerusalem.

> **1 Nephi 2: 1-2**
>
> **1** For behold, it came to pass that the Lord spake unto my father, yea, even in a dream, and said unto him: Blessed art thou Lehi, because of the things which thou hast done; and because thou hast been faithful and declared unto this people the things which I commanded thee, behold, they seek to take thy life.
>
> **2** And it came to pass that the Lord commanded my father, even in a dream, that he should take his family and depart into the wilderness.

Lehi was obedient.

> **1 Nephi 2:3-7**
>
> **3** And it came to pass that he was obedient unto the word of the Lord, wherefore he did as the Lord commanded him.
>
> **4** And it came to pass that he departed into the wilderness. And he left his house, and the land of his inheritance, and his gold, and his silver, and his precious things, and took nothing with him, save it were his family, and provisions, and tents, and departed into the wilderness.
>
> **5** And he came down by the borders near the shore of the Red Sea; and he traveled in the wilderness in the borders which are nearer the Red Sea; and he did travel in the wilderness with his family, which consisted of my mother, Sariah, and my elder brothers, who were Laman, Lemuel, and Sam.

> **6** And it came to pass that when he had traveled three days in the wilderness, he pitched his tent in a valley by the side of a river of water.
>
> **7** And it came to pass that he built an altar of stones, and made an offering unto the Lord, and gave thanks unto the Lord our God.

A greater revelation is received: Lehi was filled with the spirit, which caused physical fear in his unrighteous sons.

> **1 Nephi 2:14**
>
> **14** And it came to pass that my father did speak unto them in the valley of Lemuel, with power, being filled with the Spirit, until their frames did shake before him. And he did confound them, that they durst not utter against him; wherefore, they did as he commanded them.

And Nephi cried unto the Lord, who visited him.

> **1 Nephi 2:16**
>
> **16** And it came to pass that I, Nephi, being exceedingly young, nevertheless being large in stature, and also having great desires to know of the mysteries of God, wherefore, I did cry unto the Lord; and behold he did visit me, and did soften my heart that I did believe all the words which had been spoken by my father; wherefore, I did not rebel against him like unto my brothers.

Here's the chart:

	The reception of the initial spiritual knowledge (and then personal preparation)	A greater divine revelation is received

1 Nephi 2	Lehi (and therefore his family through him) received a revelation to leave Jerusalem. (**1 Nephi 2:1-2**) Nephi was obedient. (**1 Nephi 2:3-7**)	Lehi was filled with the spirit, which caused physical fear in his unrighteous sons, (**1 Nephi 2:14**) and Nephi cried unto the Lord, who did visit him. (**1 Nephi 2:16**)
1 Nephi 3-4	Lehi (and therefore his family) received a revelation, a commandment from the Lord to send his sons back to Jerusalem to acquire the brass plates from Laban. Lehi commanded his sons; Nephi expressed his trust in the Lord and promised to be obedient to his commandments. Other preparations for success.	Nephi received further instruction and reasoning/ revelation from the Lord at the time he encounters Laban laying in the street. (**1 Nephi 4:10-17**)
1 Nephi 5	Lehi testified to Sariah that he was indeed a visionary man (in the good/prophetic sense of the word), and that the Lord had given him a land of promise. Sariah was comforted by his words. (**1 Nephi 5:4-6**) Note that though technically hearsay, Nephi included this incident as an example of his theme.	Sariah was blessed with her own testimony of the validity of the Lord's work through her husband, the prophet. (**1 Nephi 5:8**)
1 Nephi 5 (part 2)	Lehi studied the record on the brass plates. (**1 Nephi 5:10-16**)	Lehi prophesied about his seed, the plates, etc. (**1 Nephi 5:17-22**)

1 Nephi 6. Nephi's declarations and commandments to his seed regarding this particular record. Again, we note the implication in 1 Nephi 6:6 that—at the time of writing—Nephi was older, and already had children.

	The reception of the initial **spiritual knowledge** (and then personal preparation)	A greater divine **revelation is received**

| 1 Nephi 7 | Lehi (and therefore his family) received revelation to send his sons back to town for Ishmael and family. They go back. (**1 Nephi 7:-12**) | Nephi prophesied and Laman, Lemuel and others don't take it very well. Nephi prayed and his bindings were loosed. (**1 Nephi 7:15-18** |
| **1 Nephi 8, & 10** | Lehi received and recounted his vision of the Tree of Life. (**1 Nephi 8:2-37**) | Lehi prophesied of many things. (**1 Nephi 8:38 and 10:2-15**) |

1 Nephi 9; 1Nephi 10:1, 17-22 Nephi's declarations including an explanation of this set vs. Nephi's larger set of plates. Clarifications appear to be directed both to those who would also have access to the first set of plates and to those who would not.

1 Nephi 10:1

1 And now I Nephi, proceed to give an account upon these plates of my proceedings, and my reign and ministry; wherefore to proceed with mine account, I must speak somewhat of the things of my father and also of my brethren.

The concluding verse of another section of editorial statements, this is an acknowledgment by older King Nephi—as indicated by use of the word "reign"—that he includes some hearsay of his father and brothers in order to continue to teach to the theme through incidents that occurred in his life. We note that this attestation is made right in the middle of one of the examples he is giving: The initial spiritual knowledge had been received, and the writer had just begun to share the ensuing prophecies of Lehi.

Nephi testifies of the process as described in these examples:

1 Nephi 10:17-19, 22

17And it came to pass after I, Nephi, having heard all the words of my father, concerning the things which he saw in a vision, and also the things which he spake by the power of the Holy Ghost, which power he received by faith on the Son of God—and the Son of God was the Messiah who should come—I, Nephi, was desirous also that I might see, and hear, and know of these things, by the power of the Holy Ghost, which is the gift of God unto all those who diligently seek him, as well in times of old as in the time that he should manifest himself unto the children of men.

18For he is the same yesterday, today, and forever; and the way is prepared for all men from the foundation of the world, if it so be that they repent and come unto him...

19 For he that diligently seeketh shall find; and the mysteries of God shall be unfolded unto them, by the power of the Holy Ghost, as well in these times as in times of old, and as well in times of old as in times to come; wherefore, the course of the Lord is one eternal round.

22 And the Holy Ghost giveth authority that I should speak these things, and deny them not.

And then he returns to the examples:

	The reception of the initial spiritual knowledge (and then personal preparation)	A greater divine revelation is received

1 Nephi 11-16:4	Nephi heard the recounting of Father Lehi's vision of the Tree of Life. (**1 Nephi 8.**) Note: Yes, a second lesson/example from the same starting point. Nephi desired to know the things that his father had seen, and sat pondering them. (**1 Nephi 11:1**)	Nephi received the vision of the Tree of Life and other visions, and answered some of the questions from his brothers. (**1 Nephi 11: 2 through 1 Nephi 16:4**)
1 Nephi 16 (part 2)	Lehi received revelation to move camp, receives the Liahona and occasionally there are writings on one of its spindles. (**1 Nephi 16:9-29**) Nephi follows directions/revelations from God, as given via the Liahona, in order to feed the camp. (**1 Nephi 16:30-31**)	The voice of the Lord came to the camp and chastised some of them as needed in order that they could continue as a family group. (**1 Nephi 16:25, 39**)
1 Nephi 17	Nephi is commanded to build a ship, asks about where to find ore, and he gets started (**1 Nephi 17:7-9**) Nephi testifies to his brethren about the tender mercies of the Lord to their forefathers in delivering them in their times of need. (**1 Nephi 17:23-42**), and called upon his brethren to repent (**1 Nephi 17:43-47**)	The spirit of God was with Nephi, so strong that his brethren dared not touch him. Later, when Nephi touched *them*, they witnessed further via the miracle of the shock that the Lord was with Nephi. (**1 Nephi 17:48, 52-55**)
1 Nephi 18	Nephi completes the ship. (**1 Nephi 18:4**) Lehi (and therefore the entire camp) received the revelation of a commandment from God to board the ship. (**1 Nephi 18:5-6**)	The Liahona ceased to function, and then started again when Nephi regained control of it, and of the ship. (**1 Nephi 18:21**)

1 Nephi 19 Nephi states in the chronological progression that he made the first volume(s) of the large plates soon after arrival at the promised land.

> **1 Nephi 19:1**
>
> 1 And it came to pass that the Lord commanded me, wherefore I did make plates of ore that I might engraven upon them the record of my people. And upon the plates which I made I did engraven the record of my father, and also our journeyings in the wilderness, and the prophecies of my father; and also many of mine own prophecies have I engraven upon them.

Nephi includes the purpose of the second set of plates as per the commandments he had received on the matter.

> **1 Nephi 19:3**
>
> 3 And after I had made these plates by way of commandment, I, Nephi, received a commandment that the ministry and the prophecies, the more plain and precious parts of them, should be written upon these plates; and that the things which were written should be kept for the instruction of my people, who should possess the land, and also for other wise purposes, which purposes are known unto the Lord.

Nephi promised an account of the making of the small plates at a later date, presumably so as to also be in chronological order, like the record to this point.

> **1 Nephi 19:5**
>
> 5 And an account of my making these plates shall be given hereafter; and then, behold, I proceed according to that which I have spoken; and this I do that the more sacred things may be kept for the knowledge of my people.

Nephi said that he would only write things on the plates that are sacred. Also, it appears that he was referencing his vision of the history of the world when he mentioned his concern about things that are of great worth that some may trample under their feet.

> **1 Nephi 19:6-7**
>
> **6** Nevertheless, I do not write anything upon plates save it be that I think it be sacred…
>
> **7** For the things which some men esteem to be of great worth, both to the body and soul, others set at naught and trample under their feet. Yea, even the very God of Israel do men trample under their feet; I say, trample under their feet but I would speak in other words—they set him at naught, and hearken not to the voice of his counsels.

And perhaps in part to emphasize that point—he then combined his testimony with those of other prophets about the mission of the Saviour.

> **1 Nephi 19:23-24**
>
> **23** And I did read many things unto them which were written in the books of Moses; but that I might more fully persuade them to believe in the Lord their Redeemer I did read unto them that which was written by the prophet Isaiah; for I did liken all scriptures unto us, that it might be for our profit and learning.
>
> **24** Wherefore I spake unto them, saying: Hear ye the words of the prophet, ye who are a remnant of the house of Israel, a branch who have been broken off; hear ye the words of the prophet, which were written unto all the house of

> Israel, and liken them unto yourselves, that ye may have
> hope as well as your brethren from whom ye have been
> broken off; for after this manner has the prophet written.

Now, after repeated examples of methodology describing how the Lord had delivered them these many years and against impossible odds, Nephi presented to his people, to later prophets and to

> **1 Nephi 19:19**
>
> 19 "...All the house of Israel, if it so be that they should obtain these things—

—an additional primer, with a favorite source to receive the initial spiritual knowledge, so that they might learn to receive the greater revelations that are pertinent to their particular needs.

It is an important note that Nephi introduces the Isaiah chapters specifically so that they, as a remnant of the house of Israel, might believe in "The Lord their Redeemer." This statement offers a clue as to which chapters of Isaiah that Nephi would include in the small plates: Nephi's prophesies after each section of Isaiah's words would be about the Lord's dealings with the house of Israel.

Per 1 Nephi 19:23, he taught them to be obedient to the law of Moses by teaching from the books of Moses, but in order to teach to the next level—to have a belief in Christ—Nephi specified the use of the words of Isaiah, and he gave examples to back it up. This corresponds to verse 18:

> **2 Nephi 19:18**
>
> 18 And I, Nephi, have written these things unto my people, that perhaps I might persuade them that they would remember the Lord their Redeemer.

He wanted to bolster their testimony of Christ because

Revelations 19:10

10 …the testimony of Jesus is the spirit of prophesy.

And

Proverbs 29:18

18 Where there is no vision, the people perish…

He knew that the best way to help his posterity generally was to help their prophets and other leaders specifically to receive the will of God.

At this point he returns again to the examples:

	The reception of the initial spiritual knowledge (and then personal preparation)	A greater divine revelation is received
1 Nephi 20-22	Nephi quotes **Isaiah 48-49.** The people (who at that time still included Laman and Lemuel) asked the same question that his older brethren had asked him regarding the vision of the Tree of Life. Namely: Does this pertain to spiritual things or temporal things? (**1 Nephi 20-21**)	Nephi then connected those words to other scripture and began prophesy of events beyond. (**1 Nephi 22**)
	Nephi answered questions and explained the scriptures that he had just presented, just as he would have done if in the seat of Moses in a synagogue. (**1 Nephi 22:1, See also 1 Nephi 15:31**)	

| 2 Nephi 1 through 2 Nephi 4:11 | Lehi recounted to the family the great things, the tender mercies that they had received from God in order to get to this promised land. (**2 Nephi 1: 1-5**)

This is of course the same method of reception of initial spiritual knowledge to begin the process of receiving revelation that is later also recommended by Moroni at the beginning of his famous promise. (**Moroni 10:3**) | Lehi prophesied and blessed his posterity. (**2 Nephi 1:6 through 2 Nephi 4:11**) |

2 Nephi 4:15-35 - 2 Nephi 5 signal an end to the retrospective portion of Nephi's small plates. Within this short section there are a couple of items that I wish to highlight.

2 Nephi 4:16-35 is often referred to as the Psalm of Nephi, and is described as both introspective and chiastic. Nephi had been working for some time in compiling the retrospective portion of the record of the small plates and he was almost done. It appears that he was filled with gratitude to God, thought to express it to God, and then shared it with the reader, most certainly understanding that all mankind would have times in their lives when they need to be reminded to give gratitude to God. Nephi teaches by being an example.

> **2 Nephi 5:** Nephi gave a bit of history here. The separation of his people from his wicked brethren was significant enough to include.

Though he mentioned that a temple was built, the revelations that must have been received in the process of construction and those that must have been received upon its dedication did not make the cut through the filter of

> **1 Nephi 19:3**
>
> **3** ...the ministry and prophecies, the more plain and precious parts of them.

I suggest that this is not because such revelations were unimportant, but perhaps because they did not fit into the theme/methodology that he was teaching. This is an example of Nephi the editor, making the call and drawing the line.

Near the end of 2 Nephi 5, and as promised in 1 Nephi 19:5, an accounting of the making of the small plates was included.

> **2 Nephi 5:28-31**
>
> **28** And thirty years had passed away from the time we left Jerusalem.
>
> **29** And I, Nephi, had kept the records upon my plates, which I had made, of my people thus far.
>
> **30** And it came to pass that the Lord God said unto me: Make other plates; and thou shalt engraven many things upon them which are good in my sight, for the profit of thy people.
>
> **31** Wherefore, I, Nephi, to be obedient to the commandments of the Lord, went and made these plates upon which I have engraven these things.

He puts the making of these small plates into its chronological location in the record. This means that the retrospective portion of the small plates is completed at this point. It means that the records from 1 Nephi 1 to this point in 2 Nephi 5 were all scribed upon the small plates approximately thirty to forty years after Lehi left Jerusalem.

Upon completion of the retrospective, Nephi "caused to be written" some of the words that Nephi had asked Jacob to speak to his people. (2 Nephi 11:1) The words selected for inclusion match the theme of the writings of Nephi so far, and even more specifically, include the words of Isaiah as the source for the first step in the process.

	The reception of the initial spiritual knowledge (and then personal preparation)	A greater divine revelation is received
2 Nephi 6	Jacob quoted Isaiah, who was speaking Messianic-ally. (2 Nephi 6:6-7; 16-18) See Isaiah 49:22-26	Jacob received revelation that Jerusalem has been destroyed. He prophesied that the remainder of its inhabitants were carried captive, scattered, smitten and hated, but would return. Finally, that "God would fulfill his covenants which he has made unto his children." "The Mighty God shall deliver his covenant people."
2 Nephi 6:16-18 through 2 Nephi 10	In Jacob quotes Isaiah 49:16-18 through 52:1-2 (2 Nephi 6:16-18, 7-8)	Jacob presents some of the premier scripture that we have today on the doctrine of the Atonement. (2 Nephi 9)
		The promises of the promised land—to be a land of liberty even for the Gentiles. (2 Nephi 10)

2 Nephi 11 is editorial statements by Nephi.

A few notes:

Jacob uses several of the same verses of Isaiah that had already and recently been included in the record by Nephi (1 Nephi

21:22-26), and the second, greater revelation that was received by Jacob is shorter than Nephi's, and covering some of the same items.

We also note that Nephi's second, greater revelation as listed in 1 Nephi 21:22-26 was in part resulting from questions from the congregation, including some members of which who were not as righteous as they might have been. This appears to be similar to the reason that Helaman and Shiblon received a combined total of just 92 verses of council from their father Alma, while Corianton—who was called to repentance—alone was served 91 verses . (At least as abridged by Mormon.)

There is a difference of the style of Jacob vs. Nephi, indicating a different voice in the writing. Jacob begins by quoting a couple of verses, inserts the new revelation received, and then returns and continues that passage from Isaiah, demonstrating the relevance of the older revelation to the new one. He appears to be trying less to establish Isaiah as a separate witness as Nephi did (2 Nephi 11:2-3) and was more intent on correlating the new revelation with the old.

In complimenting the hypothesis of a theme in the small plates, it appears that the reasons for Nephi's inclusion of Jacob's testimony, teachings and revelations as listed in these few chapters are two-fold:

a. The first is Jacob's buy-in: Jacob was the first student of Nephi's home-study course on becoming a better prophet, and would also be next in line as custodian and author of the small plates. Having some of his words included in the document that followed the theme was of great value.

b. The second is mentioned by Nephi in this section: There is a law of witnesses. Nephi had documented proof of it in Isaiah's day.

> **2 Nephi 18:2 (Isaiah 8:2)**
>
> 2And I took unto me faithful witnesses to record, Uriah the priest, and Zechariah the son of Jeberechiah.

This continued to be in practice when the Saviour was in the land of Jerusalem:

> **Matthew 18:16**
>
> 16 But if he will not hear thee, then take with thee one or two more, that in the mouth of two or three witnesses every word may be established.

And it continues in this dispensation.

> **Doctrine and Covenants 6:28**
>
> 28 And now, behold, I give unto you, and also unto my servant Joseph, the keys of this gift, which shall bring to light this ministry; and in the mouth of two or three witnesses shall every word be established.

Nephi understood its importance. He stated:

> **2 Nephi 11:2-3**
>
> 2 And now I, Nephi, write more of the words of Isaiah, for my soul delighteth in his words. For I will liken his

words unto my people, and I will send them forth unto all my children, for he verily saw my Redeemer, even as I have seen him.

3 And my brother, Jacob, also has seen him as I have seen him; wherefore, I will send their words forth unto my children to prove unto them that my words are true. Wherefore, by the words of three, God hath said, I will establish my word. Nevertheless, God sendeth more witnesses, and he proveth all his words. He does this because he delights in "proving ...the truth of the coming of Christ", that "all things that have been given by God from the beginning... are typifying of him" and that "save Christ should come all men should perish."

Isaiah had seen the Lord, Nephi had seen the Lord, and Jacob had seen the Lord. Nephi cited the other two to prove his words. He might have also mentioned that Lehi saw the Lord.

1 Nephi 1:8

8 And being thus overcome with the Spirit, he was carried away in a vision, even that he saw the heavens open, and he thought he saw God sitting upon his throne, surrounded with numberless concourses of angels in the attitude of singing and praising their God.

While Lehi was alive, the brass plates and Lehi were the other two witnesses to whom Nephi appealed to prove his words.

1 Nephi 22:30-31

30 Wherefore, my brethren, I would that ye should consider that the things which have been written upon the plates of brass are true; and they testify that a man must be obedient to the commandments of God.

31 Wherefore, ye need not suppose that I and my father are the only ones that have testified, and also taught them. Wherefore, if ye shall be obedient to the commandments, and endure to the end, ye shall be saved at the last day. And thus it is. Amen.

Nephi's change from Lehi to Jacob as another witness to prove his words demonstrates the importance to him of having a living witness. By extension, this demonstrates the need and importance of having a living prophet (and revelation) to prove his words.

Here is the next section of examples:

	The reception of the initial spiritual knowledge (and then personal preparation)	A greater divine revelation is received
2 Nephi 12-24,25, 26 & 30	Nephi quotes **Isaiah 2-14** (**2 Nephi 12-24**)	Nephi prophesies of events up to and including the first coming of Christ, including to his people., and then briefly to the second coming of Christ—with focus on the Jews to believe in Christ. He then testifies of the importance of focus on Christ in our teachings—even though they were instructed to obey the law of Moses. (**2 Nephi 25**) Nephi prophesies of the coming of Christ to the Nephites, of the signs and destruction that occur, of their eventual apostasy, of the Gentiles smiting them, and the Gentiles' many false churches. Nephi teaches that the covenants of the Gospel are also for the Gentiles and all who receive/accept the Gospel. Nephi prophesies the gospel will cause a division among the people, then millennial reign of the Lord will occur.(**2 Nephi 26 & 30**)

Note that **2 Nephi 27-29** will be discussed in the chapter entitled "The Next Witness." Suffice it for now to say that later in this work it will be demonstrated that these chapters also follow Nephi's theme.

Before we begin Nephi's closing remarks, we note that the pattern was also followed by other writers of the small plates of Nephi:

The Book of Jacob followed the pattern that Nephi set. It appears that Jacob, noting that Nephi (and Lehi) had referenced the allegory of Zenos (1 Nephi 10:12, 1 Nephi 15:7, 1 Nephi 19:24, 2 Nephi 3:5) was inspired to its study. Jacob included it in the record, along with the greater revelations that he had received through it.

	The reception of the initial spiritual knowledge (and then personal preparation)	**A greater divine revelation is received**
Jacob 4:10-18, 5-6	Jacob prepares the people to receive revelation though him. (**Jacob 4:10-18**) Jacob quotes Zenos' allegory of the olive vineyard—the epic history—past present and future of God's merciful dealings with his covenant people. (**Jacob 5**)	Jacob's prophecy began simply: "Behold this is my prophesy—-that the things which the prophet Zenos spake concerning the house of Israel, in which he likened them unto a tame olive tree, must surely come to pass." (**Jacob 6**)

The Book of Enos followed the pattern that Nephi had set. Enos and his father Jacob had custody of the small plates for some 124 years (Jacob 1:1; Enos 1:25, indicating that Enos had a good long life, and that they—

> **Enos 1:19**
>
> 19 ...went among the people prophesying many things to come.

Perhaps because the small plates of Nephi were finite in space (see Omni v.30) Enos had but one significant personal anecdote to include: The event selected fits the pattern that Nephi had established—in fact, the incident fit that pattern three times. We can conclude that it was selected from among his undoubtedly numerous prophecies and spiritual experiences of his long life because it expressly fit the pattern.

	The reception of the initial spiritual knowledge (and then personal preparation)	A greater divine revelation is received
Enos 1	Taught the gospel by his father, his soul hungered and he cried in mighty prayer. (Enos 1:1-4)	He received revelation of the remission of his sins. (Enos v.5-8) He received assurance from the Lord that he will visit the Nephites according to their worthiness. (Enos v.9-10) He received a covenant—like his forefathers had received—that the records would be preserved to bring forth to the Lamanites in due time. (Enos v.11-18)

By appreciating Nephi's theme, we can better comprehend how to

1 Nephi 19:23

"...liken all scriptures unto us..."

CHAPTER 14

Back Cover of Nephi

As other chapters of this work demonstrate, each of the three editors of *The Book of Mormon* incorporate near their closing an "intent"—as Moroni called it in referring to the closing remarks of his father Mormon, (Mormon 8:5)—or objective for the use of the testament as written. Each objective is different, due in part to the fact that each is written to different—but not necessarily mutually exclusive—groups of people.

Nephi, the earliest editor of *The Book of Mormon*, and editor in-the-blind for the balance of small plates of Nephi, also included a purpose for his writings, which spans most of two chapters. When 2 Nephi 31-32 is legitimately compared to 1 Nephi 1, especially in light of the theme of Nephi, it becomes plain that Nephi's objective for the use of the information that he has provided to us stems from what he had promised from the beginning.

> **1 Nephi 1:20**
>
> **20** ...behold, I, Nephi, will show unto you that the tender mercies of the Lord are over all those whom he hath chosen, because of their faith, to make them mighty even unto the power of deliverance.

These two chapters are Nephi's explanation of the best use of the thematic training that he had provided—not only the prophets and leaders of his people, but to all who seek this learning in this dispensation—are stated with clarity and candor. It would appear that these chapters are often misunderstood because the catechumen has not captured the theme of Nephi's small plates, which leads to not understanding the primary audience that Nephi is writing to.

As previously established, tender mercies are revelations, gifts from God to help us along our path. All tender mercies are revelations in one aspect or another and all revelations are tender mercies in one aspect or another.

One of the verses ends with the word "Amen" (2 Nephi 31:21). This generates a handy chapter-end. There are undoubtedly good reasons for the bi-section where it was made—and far be it from me to question the Lord's work in the matter—but in the light of Nephi's theme, even a shallow reading of these two chapters discloses that Nephi did not close his lesson with that verse, but that the two chapters together comprise one sermon. It seems to this simple student that if this instruction had not been divided into two chapters, it would be easier to understand it as a conclusion of the purpose in writing as introduced at the start of the small plates. And taking this into account, It causes this observer to wonder just a smidgen if perhaps it was purposefully designed that it should not be obvious to the casual reader.

To recap:

1. The books of 1 Nephi and 2 Nephi have a theme.

2. The first chapter of 1 Nephi is an introduction of that theme.

3. 2 Nephi 31-32 is the summation of the theme of the work, an articulate explanation of the theme to the reader, and frank

and plain lesson to the reader on how to use this information to benefit the true followers of Jesus Christ.

> **2 Nephi 31:1**
>
> 1 And now I, Nephi, make an end of my prophesyings unto you, my beloved brethren. And I cannot write but a few things, which I know must surely come to pass; neither can I write but a few of the words of my brother Jacob.

And now I, Nephi, make an end of my prophesyings unto you, my beloved brethren. This is Nephi stating that pattern that he was teaching has ended, which was to begin with a revelation and then receive revelation/prophesy based on the first truth. We can infer that he was referring to the entirety of the record to this point, since he even mentions the words of Jacob, which were included at about the middle of the document.

And I cannot write but a few things, which I know must surely come to pass; Which means he actually knows more, but either is forbidden to say;

> **2 Nephi 32:7**
>
> 7And now I, Nephi, cannot say more; the Spirit stoppeth mine utterance...

And/or it was not according to the theme he was teaching and so he thought it would be distracting.

> **2 Nephi 31:3**
>
> 3 For my soul delighteth in plainness...

...neither can I write but a few of the words of my brother Jacob. He may have already been thinking about or pre-writing this "intent" or "back cover" some time before completing many of the previous chapters.

He then makes it very clear that he is ending the main corpus and is beginning the end notes:

> **2 Nephi 31:2**
>
> 2 Wherefore, the things which I have written sufficeth me, save it be a few words which I must speak concerning the doctrine of Christ...

He prefaces his next remarks as being plain, and as clear as possible.

> **2 Nephi 31:2-3**
>
> 2 ...wherefore, I shall speak unto you plainly, according to the plainness of my prophesying.
>
> 3 For my soul delighteth in plainness; for after this manner doth the Lord God work among the children of men. For the Lord God giveth light unto the understanding; for he speaketh unto men according to their language, unto their understanding.

And he mentions plainness thrice more at the completion of this sermon:

> **2 Nephi 32:7**
>
> 7 And now I, Nephi, cannot say more; the Spirit stoppeth mine utterance, and I am left to mourn because of the unbelief, and the wickedness, and the ignorance, and the

stiffneckedness of men; for they will not search knowledge, nor understand great knowledge, when it is given unto them in plainness, even as plain as word can be.

2 Nephi 33:3, 5-6

3 But I, Nephi, have written what I have written, and I esteem it as of great worth...

5 And it speaketh harshly against sin, according to the plainness of the truth...

6 I glory in plainness...

It is important to note that he is not suddenly talking to someone who has no understanding of the gospel, that he has not pivoted to speak directly and only to the seven year-old Primary class who are preparing for baptism. Sometimes these verses are taken out of context and used for other worthy purposes, like the teaching of basic principles and ordinance of the gospel. It is evident however that plainness is a relative term: Relative—not to a teacher who flaunts his understanding before the heathen masses—but to the student to whom Nephi has already described just how these things can be made plain:

2 Nephi 25:4

4 Wherefore, hearken, O my people, which are of the house of Israel, and give ear unto my words; for because the words of Isaiah are not plain unto you, nevertheless they are plain unto all those that are filled with the spirit of prophesy. But I give unto you a prophesy, according to the spirit which is in me; wherefore I shall prophesy according to the plainness which hath been with me from the time that

> I came out from Jerusalem with my father; for behold, my soul delighteth in plainness unto my people, that they may learn.

If we look at these "end-notes" true to their placement in Nephi's writing, it is evident that Nephi is speaking *plainly* to those who have studied the previous body of work, to those who have braved through the Isaiah chapters, to those who have annotated the prophesies of Nephi and of Jacob, up to this point. Nephi is asking us to remember the theme of Nephi: that we first receive revelation either directly, through God's current prophets or through his past prophets via the scriptures, then remember that we need to ponder these things in our hearts, and then ask for and receive the greater revelation that God has for us.

2 Nephi 32:1

1 And now, behold, my beloved brethren, I suppose that ye ponder somewhat in your hearts concerning that which ye should do after ye have entered in by the way. But, behold, why do ye ponder these things in your hearts?

Although all people can benefit from the words of Nephi, he is writing to those who have matured considerably in their understanding of the gospel and have a righteous desire to improve themselves as a more useful tool in the hand of God. In essence, he is writing to those who would receive revelation to benefit themselves and others. Knowing that as a secondary benefit of his work, some of the others will learn some of the things that he has taught along the way, Nephi is writing to the serious student of the scriptures. To these adherents, he speaks as transparently as he possibly can.

In order to be as plain as possible, Nephi starts with a simple logical progression: The Lamb of God was baptized and received the

Holy Ghost, thereby demonstrating to us with exactness the course that we are to follow.

> **2 Nephi 31:4-9**
>
> 4 Wherefore, I would that ye should remember that I have spoken unto you concerning that prophet which the Lord showed unto me, that should baptize the Lamb of God, which should take away the sins of the world.
>
> 5 And now, if the Lamb of God, he being holy, should have need to be baptized by water, to fulfil all righteousness, O then, how much more need have we, being unholy, to be baptized, yea, even by water!
>
> 6 And now, I would ask of you, my beloved brethren, wherein the Lamb of God did fulfil all righteousness in being baptized by water?
>
> 7 Know ye not that he was holy? But notwithstanding he being holy, he showeth unto the children of men that, according to the flesh he humbleth himself before the Father, and witnesseth unto the Father that he would be obedient unto him in keeping his commandments.
>
> 8 Wherefore, after he was baptized with water the Holy Ghost descended upon him in the form of a dove.
>
> 9 And again, it showeth unto the children of men the straitness of the path, and the narrowness of the gate, by which they should enter, he having set the example before them.

Christ is the example to follow in all things.

Then, for clarity and plainness, Nephi scribes for us, the readers, the very words of the Father and the very words of the Son in the matter, in the way that he had received them. This is something that he had not done before in his writing to us (See chapter in this work entitled "The Next Witness" regarding 2 Nephi 27-29) and thereby demonstrates an overt example of his objective.

He starts by quoting the words of the Son:

> **2 Nephi 31:10**
>
> **10** And he said unto the children of men: Follow thou me. Wherefore, my beloved brethren, can we follow Jesus save we shall be willing to keep the commandments of the Father?

Next he quotes the words of the Father:

> **2 Nephi 31:11**
>
> **11** And the Father said: Repent ye, repent ye, and be baptized in the name of my Beloved Son.

Then he quotes the Son again:

> **2 Nephi 31:12**
>
> **12** And also, the voice of the Son came unto me, saying: He that is baptized in my name, to him will the Father give the Holy Ghost, like unto me; wherefore, follow me, and do the things which ye have seen me do.

Then in verse thirteen Nephi testifies—which we will return to shortly. But to continue the pattern *in plainness*: He quotes the Son again:

2 Nephi 31:14-15

14 But, behold, my beloved brethren, thus came the voice of the Son unto me, saying: After ye have repented of your sins, and witnessed unto the Father that ye are willing to keep my commandments, by the baptism of water, and have received the baptism of fire and of the Holy Ghost, and can speak with a new tongue, yea, even with the tongue of angels, and after this should deny me, it would have been better for you that ye had not known me.

And finally, he again quotes the Father:

15 And I heard a voice from the Father, saying: Yea, the words of my Beloved are true and faithful. He that endureth to the end, the same shall be saved.

While explaining the importance of the basic principles and ordinances of the gospel of Jesus Christ, Nephi has also established and has been very plain about a pattern of speaking the words of Christ. Along with this, Nephi testifies:

2 Nephi 31:13

13 Wherefore, my beloved brethren, I know that if ye shall follow the Son, with full purpose of heart, acting no hypocrisy and no deception before God, but with real intent, repenting of your sins, witnessing unto the Father that ye are willing to take upon you the name of Christ, by baptism—yea, by following your Lord and your Savior down into the water, according to his word, behold, then shall ye receive the Holy Ghost; yea, then cometh the baptism of fire and of the Holy Ghost; and then can ye speak with the tongue of angels, and shout praises unto the Holy One of Israel.

I know… I testify as if in court, based on personal knowledge.

Repenting of your sins, witnessing unto the Father that ye are willing to take upon you the name of Christ, by baptism—yea, by following your Lord and your Savior down into the water, according to his word, behold, then shall ye receive the Holy Ghost… Faith, repentance, baptism and the Gift of the Holy Ghost: All things included in the fourth Article of Faith:

These are important and basic concepts of the gospel. These things usually receive so much attention that we often skip the conclusion of this verse. But—understanding that Nephi is specifically teaching leaders among the followers of Christ, these things are just the example and precursor to his main point of not only this two-chapter sermon but the underlying theme of all of his writing since the first chapter of 1 Nephi.

It is an "if-then, then, then, then" statement:

> **2 Nephi 31:13**
>
> **13** …*If* ye shall follow the Son… *then* shall ye receive the Holy Ghost; yea, *then* cometh the baptism of fire and of the Holy Ghost; and *then* can ye speak with the tongue of angels, and *(then)* shout praises unto the Holy One of Israel.

Then cometh the baptism of fire and of the Holy Ghost.

> **Book of Mormon Central, KnoWhy #60, March 23, 2016. https://knowhy.bookofmormoncentral.org/knowhy/ what-is-it-to-speak-with-the-tongue-of-angels**
>
> "This shares the similar imagery with Isaiah's vision, quoted by Nephi, where a seraph (*sārāp*)—meaning "fiery one"—purges Isaiah of his sins by placing a hot coal to

his mouth. Isaiah then becomes a member of the heavenly hosts and speaks/participates in the council. In other words, after being cleansed from sin by fire, Isaiah spoke 'with the tongue of angels'."

We refer to Isaiah's writing, when he was called to prophesy, as had been quoted recently by Nephi.

2 Nephi 16:5-8 (see also Isaiah 6:5-8)

5 Then said I: Wo is unto me! for I am undone; because I am a man of unclean lips; and I dwell in the midst of a people of unclean lips; for mine eyes have seen the King, the Lord of Hosts.

6 Then flew one of the seraphim unto me, having a live coal in his hand, which he had taken with the tongs from off the altar;

7 And he laid it upon my mouth, and said: Lo, this has touched thy lips; and thine iniquity is taken away, and thy sin purged.

8 Also I heard the voice of the Lord, saying: Whom shall I send, and who will go for us? Then I said: Here am I; send me.

And then can ye speak with the tongue of angels, and shout praises unto the Holy One of Israel. This also refers to that chapter wherein Isaiah recounts receiving his calling as a prophet. Speaking with the tongue of angels, as later made plain by Nephi, means to speak the words of Christ.

> **2 Nephi 32:2-3**
>
> 2Do ye not remember that I said unto you that after ye had received the Holy Ghost ye could speak with the tongue of angels? And now, how could ye speak with the tongue of angels save it were by the Holy Ghost?
>
> 3 Angels speak by the power of the Holy Ghost; wherefore, they speak the words of Christ.

Access to these words and the calling to speak them is to be a prophet, and to prophesy. Indeed prophets and angels serve similar functions, in that they are corollary witnesses to the Holy Ghost: Jacob even quotes both in the same sentence:

> **2 Nephi 25:19**
>
> 19 For according to the words of the prophets, the Messiah cometh in six hundred years from the time that my father left Jerusalem; and according to the words of the prophets, and also the word of the angel of God, his name shall be Jesus Christ, the Son of God.

As another example: How often have you heard a new revelation spoken from the pulpit by a prophet of God, that, instead of being shockingly new, it felt familiar, comfortable, and—dare I say—anti-climactic? Is it not because you were in tune with the Holy Ghost, and that he had already prepared you and spoken the truths to you in the matter?

Nephi's multiple mentioning of the voice/words of the Father and voice/words of the Son is not insignificant as an example of his main point of these closing remarks. If it would not have been mistaken for being self-aggrandizing, Nephi might have more simply said: "I'm a prophet of God. I speak the words of Christ. Follow Christ, so that you can do what I do."

1 Nephi 31:19-21, 2 Nephi 32:1

19 And now, my beloved brethren, after ye have gotten into this strait and narrow path, I would ask if all is done? Behold, I say unto you, Nay; for ye have not come thus far save it were by the word of Christ with unshaken faith in him, relying wholly upon the merits of him who is mighty to save.

20 Wherefore, ye must press forward with a steadfastness in Christ, having a perfect brightness of hope, and a love of God and of all men. Wherefore, if ye shall press forward, feasting upon the word of Christ, and endure to the end, behold, thus saith the Father: Ye shall have eternal life.

21 And now, behold, my beloved brethren, this is the way; and there is none other way nor name given under heaven whereby man can be saved in the kingdom of God. And now, behold, this is the doctrine of Christ, and the only and true doctrine of the Father, and of the Son, and of the Holy Ghost, which is one God, without end. Amen.

1And now, behold, my beloved brethren, I suppose that ye ponder somewhat in your hearts concerning that which ye should do after ye have entered in by the way. But, behold, why do ye ponder these things in your hearts?

I would ask if all is done. Nephi is knowingly overlaying a couple of lessons here, and he wants the student of his work to realize that the first part, about being baptized and having been set in the straight and narrow path is not a logical processional conclusion.

Feasting on the words of Christ is exactly the process that Nephi has been describing since the beginning of his work: The word of Christ may come through the current prophets, through previous prophets via the scriptures, from angels, and—as manifest by Nephi—from Christ himself. We demonstrate faith by preparing ourselves through obedience, and through meditating on and praying about the words of Christ that we have been given so far, so that we can be open to receiving more and willing to react favorably to the additional information that we receive. This is feasting.

With the vision that Jacob, and those who followed him generation upon generation as the prophets and leaders of Nephi's people are the primary addressees, he continued:

> **2 Nephi 32:2**
>
> 2Do ye not remember that I said unto you that after ye had received the Holy Ghost ye could speak with the tongue of angels? And now, how could ye speak with the tongue of angels save it were by the Holy Ghost?

In other words, "You are called to be prophets and leaders, and therefore are called speak the words of Christ as do angels, by the power of the Holy Ghost."

> **2 Nephi 32:3**
>
> 3 Angels speak by the power of the Holy Ghost; wherefore, they speak the words of Christ. Wherefore, I said unto you, feast upon the words of Christ; for behold, the words of Christ will tell you all things what ye should do.

Speaking words implies the teaching and leading of others, not simply someone talking to himself. Perhaps not all are called to lead in this outward fashion, but many are. Leadership as well as other talents are essential within the church, just as Paul describes it as the body of Christ:

> **1 Corinthians 12:12, 14-15, 26-27**
>
> **12** For as the body is one, and hath many members, and all the members of that one body, being many, are one body: so also is Christ.
>
> **14** For the body is not one member, but many.
>
> **15** If the foot shall say, Because I am not the hand, I am not of the body; is it therefore not of the body?
>
> **26** And whether one member suffer, all the members suffer with it; or one member be honoured, all the members rejoice with it.
>
> **27** Now ye are the body of Christ, and members in particular.

"Angels speak by the power of the Holy Ghost; wherefore they speak the words of Christ." Nephi is speaking in plainness. Angels reveal truth. They are authorized and commissioned to speak the words that Christ has given them to speak at that time. And in verse 2, Nephi's students are instructed to seek out this gift which comes through the power of the Holy Ghost. Revelation is the tender mercy by which Nephi and his family were delivered through all their peril.

> **1 Nephi 1:20**
>
> **20** ... But behold, I, Nephi, will show unto you that the tender mercies of the Lord are over all those whom he hath chosen, because of their faith, to make them mighty even unto the power of deliverance.

It is the power by which Moses brought the children of Israel across the Red Sea on dry ground.

> **Doctrine and Covenants 8:2-4**
>
> **2** Yea, behold, I will tell you in your mind and in your heart, by the Holy Ghost, which shall come upon you and which shall dwell in your heart.
>
> **3** Now, behold, this is the spirit of revelation; behold, this is the spirit by which Moses brought the children of Israel through the Red Sea on dry ground.
>
> **4** Therefore this is thy gift; apply unto it, and blessed art thou, for it shall deliver you...

At this point, Nephi shares that it will take some effort on the disciple's part to draw upon the well of revelation.

> **2 Nephi 32:4-5**
>
> **4** Wherefore, now after I have spoken these words, if ye cannot understand them it will be because ye ask not, neither do ye knock; wherefore, ye are not brought into the light, but must perish in the dark.
>
> **5** For behold, again I say unto you that if ye will enter in by the way, and receive the Holy Ghost, it will show unto you all things what ye should do.

He tells the reader what he might be lacking to be successful. Study, ponder, pray *and ask*. Nephi had seen in vision that many, then later nearly all of his people, the Nephites, would perish in the dark, having rejected the prophets.

> **2 Nephi 32:6-7**
>
> **6** Behold, this is the doctrine of Christ, and there will be no more doctrine given until after he shall manifest himself unto you in the flesh. And when he shall manifest himself unto you in the flesh, the things which he shall say unto you shall ye observe to do.

As if to make up for the fact that writing in reformed Egyptian precludes him from the use of multiple exclamation points, Nephi takes it upon him to repeat the lesson twice, ending with the same phrase:

> **2 Nephi 31:21**
>
> **21** And now, behold, my beloved brethren, this is the way; and there is none other way nor name given under heaven whereby man can be saved in the kingdom of God. And now, *behold this is the doctrine of Christ,* and the only and true doctrine of the Father, and of the Son, and of the Holy Ghost, which is one God, without end. Amen.

> **2 Nephi 32:6**
>
> **6** *Behold, this is the doctrine of Christ,* and there will be no more doctrine given until after he shall manifest himself unto you in the flesh. And when he shall manifest himself unto you in the flesh, the things which he shall say unto you shall ye observe to do.

And, as if Nephi needs my help, my keyboard includes punctuation:

Behold, this is the doctrine of Christ!!!

> **2 Nephi 32:7**
>
> 7 And now I, Nephi, cannot say more; the Spirit stoppeth mine utterance, and I am left to mourn because of the unbelief, and the wickedness, and the ignorance, and the stiffneckedness of men; for they will not search knowledge, nor understand great knowledge, when it is given unto them in plainness, even as plain as word can be.

Nephi is stopped from saying more, and acknowledges that there will be plenty of those who will have access to his words and teachings as plain as they are, who foolishly will not accept them nor do the work to obtain the blessings of revelation as spelled out.

He does however, close this out by reiterating the message from verse four, namely, to pray.

> **2 Nephi 32:8-9**
>
> 8 And now, my beloved brethren, I perceive that ye ponder still in your hearts; and it grieveth me that I must speak concerning this thing. For if ye would hearken unto the Spirit which teacheth a man to pray, ye would know that ye must pray....
>
> 9 But behold, I say unto you that ye must pray always, and not faint...

In his final words to us, Nephi testifies of the value of this writing:

> **2 Nephi 33:3**
>
> 3 ...I, Nephi, have written what I have written, and I esteem it as of great worth...

He testifies that all can benefit from these words because they are the words of Christ, and testifies that he was commanded by Christ to write these things:

> **2 Nephi 33:10**
>
> 10 ...hearken unto these words and believe in Christ; and if ye believe not in these words believe in Christ. And if ye shall believe in Christ ye will believe in these words, for they are the words of Christ, and he hath given them unto me...

His witness is also two-edged: He testifies that the words he has written will condemn those who do not observe them.

> **2 Nephi 33:10, 14-15**
>
> 11 And if they are not the words of Christ, judge ye—for Christ will show unto you, with power and great glory, that they are his words, at the last day; and you and I shall stand face to face before his bar; and ye shall know that I have been commanded of him to write these things...
>
> 14 And you that will not partake of the goodness of God, and respect the words of the Jews, and also my words, and the words which shall proceed forth out of the mouth of the Lamb of God, behold, I bid you an everlasting farewell, for these words shall condemn you at the last day.
>
> 15 For what I seal on earth, shall be brought against you at the judgement bar; for thus hath the Lord commanded me, and I must obey. Amen.

Through Nephi, the Lord blessed the people of Nephi and those who would be saints in this dispensation with a primer on receiving revelation. This was written for the prophets, and for all of us. Paralleling the quotation by

> **Werner Heisenberg, (the father of quantum mechanics)**
>
> The first gulp of natural sciences will make you an atheist, but at the bottom of the glass God is waiting for you,",

—the perceived shortcomings of Nephi as a writer are actually clues to his brilliance in following the theme. Nephi created a chronological organization of example after example of his theme. He understood that the greatest blessing that he could leave was not simply historical record, but a workable method to help us receive the tender mercies that can deliver us through our current trials.

He began by assembling a finite amount of plates together and referred to incidents recorded first on his larger set of plates. He knew from the outset that he could not engrave upon them enough fish for the student to live on, so he used the space to teach the student how to fish. The multidimensional scripture that he inscribed on plates of ore was indeed

> **1 Nephi 19:23**
>
> 23 ...for our profit and learning.

When we investigate Nephi's editorial sections of his record, identify each of their specific purpose and then highlight the balance, the pattern is clear: Nephi didn't want his people—or us—to be spiritually blind, so he created an instruction manual for the prophets and for all who would receive revelation.

1 Nephi 22:20

20 ...and the Lord will surely prepare a way for his people...

CHAPTER 15

Next Witness

We would be remiss in our study of the theme of Nephi if we did not allow for a separate essay covering the anomaly identified as 2 Nephi 27-29.

There are similarities when comparing these chapters to the balance of 1 Nephi and 2 Nephi. Like the balance of *The Book of Mormon*, this section is scripture, and contains the gospel of Jesus Christ.

And—like the other sections of Nephi where Isaiah is quoted—it too was included in *The Book of Mormon* that we should learn from it.

The following table is set up just as the prior tables, and demonstrates that this section follows the pattern of the Nephi's theme as explained in the preceding chapter with that title.

	The reception of the initial spiritual knowledge (and then personal preparation)	A greater divine revelation is received
2 Nephi 27-29	Isaiah 29 is quoted (2 **Nephi 27: 2-5, 15, 19, 25-35.**)	Revelation regarding the offering of the first 116 pages of manuscript to Professor Charles Anton.
		Revelation regarding the three witnesses. Instruction specifically directed to the unlearned man who was called of God to translate the record. (**2 Nephi 27:1, 6-14, 20-23**)
		Prophesies and explanation of many false churches in the last dispensation, of the lack of belief in miracles, of pride and corruption. Prophesies of gathering of the house of Israel to the lands of their possessions. (**2 Nephi 28-29**)

The foundational words of Christ for this section of scripture come from the writings of Isaiah, as does much of 2 Nephi; in this case, specifically Isaiah 29, as found in 2 Nephi 27. 2 Nephi 28 & 29 are explanations and new revelation pursuant to the pattern that Nephi had implemented from the beginning.

In this essay I will present evidence in support of the following hypothesis:

During the process of translation of this part of *The Book of Mormon*, Joseph Smith was apparently commissioned by God to and did in fact include his personal buy-in, his voice that the theme of Nephi was correct; a witness and testimony. That within the text of *The Book of Mormon*—specifically the section we know as 2 Nephi 27-29—he inserted a conveyance of new revelation that was separate from the work that Nephi had provided on the golden plates; and that he wrote it according to the pattern of the theme of Nephi, but in a different voice.

In order to do this we will partition the effort into a few general segments, and then into individual elements. We will:

Item 1: Evaluate evidence that these chapters were inserted, Including when in the translation process.

Item 2: Explore the precedent set to allow for and inspire such an act: The relevance and pattern of Nephi's primary apprentice, Jacob.

Item 3: Evaluate evidence that these chapters were inserted, including location in the text.

Item 4: Examine by chart

   a. the pattern of the relationship of Nephi's writing compared to KJV Isaiah,

   b. the pattern of the relationship of Jacob's writing compared to KJV Isaiah and

   c. the pattern of the relationship of the next witness' writing to KJV Isaiah.

Item 5: Explore various evidence that these chapters were written in a new voice.

Item 6: Examine the one verse in this section that uniquely points to Nephi, and why it fits with the way that Joseph Smith conveyed this revelation in the text.

Item 7: Eliminate possible writers and identify the actual writer of this section of scripture.

Then we will:

- Explore the ramifications of this information with regard to understanding these particular chapters and clarifying the thematic message of Nephi, both in the immediately adjacent sections and globally in the conclusion section of his work.

- Consider the importance of this new voice in other editorial verses found throughout *The Book of Mormon*.
- Discuss the understanding that this evidence provides in the revelatory process of translation which Joseph Smith experienced, and that it was as if Nephi taught Joseph Smith how to receive revelation, just as he had written to teach the future leaders of the Nephites to receive revelation. We will discuss the importance of these chapters as revelation of this dispensation, and how this revealed information clarified the role of Joseph Smith in the restoration of the gospel.

Item 1: *Evaluate evidence that these chapters were inserted, including at what point during the translation process.*

It is important to remember that the books of Mosiah through Moroni were translated first, and the small plates of Nephi were the last part of *The Book of Mormon* to be translated.

> **Book of Mormon Central, KnoWhy #503, February 22, 20196.**
>
> **https://knowhy.bookofmormoncentral.org/knowhy/how-does-the-mosiah-first-translation-sequence-strengthen-faith**
>
> Many readers of *The Book of Mormon* naturally assume that Joseph Smith translated its books in the order that we find them today, that is, beginning with the Title Page, and then translating 1 Nephi 1:1 through Moroni 10:34. It may be surprising to learn that the books from the small plates of Nephi (1 Nephi through Words of Mormon) almost certainly came last in the translation process, after the completion of Mormon's abridgment of the large plates of Nephi (Mosiah through 4 Nephi) followed by the books of Mormon, Ether, Moroni and the Title Page.

This unexpected translation sequence is because the first 116 pages of *The Book of Mormon's* translation—which contained a record called the Book of Lehi—were lost by Martin Harris in the summer of 1828. When the translation resumed in April 1829, it appears Joseph Smith picked up where he had left off, namely in the early chapters of Mosiah, rather than retranslating Mormon's record from the beginning.

Thankfully, the Lord had a plan, more than two millennia in advance, to compensate for the lost Book of Lehi. Important ancient documents were often "doubled" and backup copies provided a safeguard against loss or damage. In keeping with this ancient practice, the Lord told Nephi to keep two sets of records—a historical and public record on his large plates, and a shorter, more spiritually focused record on his small plates. Thus Nephi's small plates contained an abbreviated account of that was on the book of Lehi, which was recorded in Nephi's large plates (see 1 Nephi 19:1). Hundreds of years later, the Lord inspired Mormon to append Nephi's small plates to his own abridgement (see Words of Mormon 1:3-7). This explains why the books from the small plates would show up last rather than first in the translation process—that was their order on the plates themselves. When it came time to publish *The Book of Mormon*, Joseph and Oliver moved the transcription of Nephi's small plates to the beginning of the text, where it provided an ideal starting point and replacement for the lost book of Lehi.

This means in the timeline of the perspective of Joseph Smith, Moroni first set the precedent of inserting in the translation process with one's own revelation. As one of a few examples we could cite, Moroni—though short on space on the plates—opted to share a particular revelation to us, which we now know as Ether 12.

> **Ether 12: 5-6**
>
> 5 And it came to pass that Ether did prophesy great and marvelous things unto the people, which they did not believe, because they saw them not.
>
> 6 And now, I, Moroni, would speak somewhat concerning these things...

After Ether 12, Moroni continued again with the balance of the translation of the history of the Jaredites.

Item 2: *Explore the precedent set to allow for and inspire such an act: The relevance and pattern of Nephi's primary apprentice, Jacob.* Even more directly pertinent, is the standard set by Jacob.

To begin with, Nephi stated in no uncertain terms an important purpose in his writing.

> **1 Nephi 19:18-19**
>
> 18 And I, Nephi, have written these things unto my people, that perhaps I might persuade them that they would remember the Lord their Redeemer.
>
> 19 Wherefore, I speak unto all the house of Israel, if it so be that they should obtain these things.

He accomplishes this task not only by his own testimony, but he appeals to the testimony of Lehi, who saw our Redeemer (1 Nephi 1: 8-10) and also to the testimony of Isaiah who saw our Redeemer.

> **2 Nephi 11:2**
>
> 2 And now I, Nephi, write more of the words of Isaiah, for my soul delighteth in his words. For I will liken his

> words unto my people, and I will send them forth unto all my children, for he verily saw my Redeemer, even as I have seen him.

Nephi included several chapters of Lehi's prophesies and testimony as found near the beginning of 1 Nephi and near the beginning of 2 Nephi. He included several chapters of prophesies and testimony of Isaiah as found near the end of 1 Nephi and in the middle of 2 Nephi. Then, apparently as an opportune replacement of Lehi's live witness, Nephi included a few chapters of Jacob's prophesies and testimony as found starting in 2 Nephi 6.

2 Nephi 11:3

3And my brother, Jacob, also has seen him as I have seen him; wherefore, I will send their words forth unto my children to prove unto them that my words are true. Wherefore, by the words of three, God hath said, I will establish my word. Nevertheless, God sendeth more witnesses, and he proveth all his words.

Nephi mentioned the need for special witnesses of the Savior and in so doing explained why Jacob had been asked to add something to the text. Joseph Smith also saw the Savior and Redeemer of the world.

Joseph Smith—History 1:17

17 ...I saw two Personages, whose brightness and glory defy all description, standing above me in the air. One of them spake unto me, calling me by name and said, pointing to the other—*This is My Beloved Son. Hear Him!*

And as a special witness of the Lord Jesus Christ, it was more a necessity than an opportunity that Joseph Smith should add his testimony to the translated text. Like Jacob had been, Joseph Smith was now the prime student and the inheritor of the obligations and accountabilities that had rested with Nephi. This is not unlike Isaiah's "burden".

> **2 Nephi 23:1**
>
> 1 The burden of Babylon, which Isaiah the son of Amoz did see.

Joseph Smith, as translator, special witness of the Lord Jesus Christ, and prophet of God was equally burdened with receiving revelations and the duty to disseminate them to the people of this dispensation. God had indeed sent another witness, and so he would testify.

Item 3: *Evaluate evidence that these chapters were inserted, including location in the text.*

Reading the end of chapter 26 followed immediately by the beginning of chapter 30 demonstrates that chapter 30 is simply a continuation of the thought started in 26. Since *The Book of Mormon* was originally written without chapter headings, without chapters, and even without verses, if we remove some of these extra markings it is easier to see how smoothly the end of 2 Nephi 26 transitions to the beginning of 2 Nephi 30.

> **2 Nephi 26:27-33; 30: 1-8**
>
> Hath he commanded any that they should not partake of his salvation? Behold I say unto you, Nay; but he hath given it free for all men; and he hath commanded his people that they should persuade all men to repentance.

Behold, hath the Lord commanded any that they should not partake of his goodness? Behold I say unto you, Nay; but all men are privileged the one like unto the other, and none are forbidden.

He commandeth that there shall be no priestcrafts; for, behold, priestcrafts are that men preach and set themselves up for a light unto the world, that they may get gain and praise of the world; but they seek not the welfare of Zion.

Behold, the Lord hath forbidden this thing; wherefore, the Lord God hath given a commandment that all men should have charity, which charity is love.

And except they should have charity they were nothing. Wherefore, if they should have charity they would not suffer the laborer in Zion to perish.

But the laborer in Zion shall labor for Zion; for if they labor for money they shall perish.

And again, the Lord God hath commanded that men should not murder; that they should not lie; that they should not steal; that they should not take the name of the Lord their God in vain; that they should not envy; that they should not have malice; that they should not contend one with another; that they should not commit whoredoms; and that they should do none of these things; for whoso doeth them shall perish.

For none of these iniquities come of the Lord; for he doeth that which is good among the children of men; and he doeth nothing save it be plain unto the children of men; and he inviteth them all to come unto him and partake of his goodness; and he denieth none that come unto him, black and white, bond and free, male and female; and he remembereth the heathen; and all are alike unto God, both Jew and Gentile.

And now behold, my beloved brethren, I would not suffer that ye should suppose that ye are more righteous than the Gentiles shall be. For behold, except ye shall keep the commandments of God ye shall all likewise perish; and because of the words which have been spoken ye need not suppose that the Gentiles are utterly destroyed.

For behold, I say unto you that as many of the Gentiles as will repent are the covenant people of the Lord; and as many of the Jews as will not repent shall be cast off; for the Lord coventanteth with none save it be with them that repent and believe in his Son, who is the Holy One of Israel.

And now, I would prophesy somewhat more concerning the Jews and the Gentiles. For after the book of which I have spoken shall come forth, and be written unto the Gentiles, and sealed up again unto the Lord, there shall be many which shall believe the words which are written; and they shall carry them forth unto the remnant of our seed.

And then shall the remnant of our seed know concerning us, how that we came out from Jerusalem, and that they are descendants of the Jews.

And the gospel of Jesus Christ shall be declared among them; wherefore, they shall be restored unto the knowledge of their fathers, and also to the knowledge of Jesus Christ, which was had among their fathers.

And then shall they rejoice; for they shall know that it is a blessing unto them from the hand of God; and their scales of darkness shall begin to fall from their eyes; and many generations shall not pass away among them, save they shall be a pure and a delightsome people.

And it shall come to pass that the Jews which are scattered also shall begin to believe in Christ; and they shall begin to gather in upon the face of the land; and as many as shall believe in Christ shall also become a delightsome people.

> And it shall come to pass that the Lord God shall commence his work among all nations, kindreds, tongues, and people, to bring about the restoration of his people upon the earth.

In order to demonstrate how seamlessly the thought or lesson continues from the end of 2 Nephi 26, to the beginning of 2 Nephi 30, I actually also omitted one identifier phrase which I will later show is a transitional phrase from one speaker/writer in 2 Nephi 27-29 back to the original for whom these plates were named.

Here is the complete verse, which fits correctly into the footprint of the eighth paragraph/verse above, and with the identifier phrase in *italics*.

> **2 Nephi 30:1**
>
> 1And now behold, my beloved brethren, I *would speak unto you; for I, Nephi,* would not suffer that ye should suppose that ye are more righteous than the Gentiles shall be. For behold, except ye shall keep the commandments of God ye shall all likewise perish; and because of the words which have been spoken ye need not suppose that the Gentiles are utterly destroyed.

The phrase "I Nephi" is not used at all in the previous three chapters, but is now needed as a segue to and an identifier of the change of speakers/return to the original speaker.

We should keep in mind that there are many, perhaps most of the cases when chapter endings and chapter beginnings were selected for later printings of *The Book of Mormon* corresponding with the endings and beginnings of distinct thoughts/lessons, and that one chapter does not, and does not necessarily need to segue this well into the next. Their insertion into the middle of another lesson spotlight that these three chapters were intended to be found as a separate corpus.

Item 4: *Examine by chart the pattern of verse-to-verse relationship of Nephi's writing compared to King James Version- Isaiah, the pattern of verse-to verse relationship of Jacob's writing compared to KJV Isaiah and the pattern of verse-to-verse relationship of the next witness' writing to KJV Isaiah.*

The use of a chart is a simple tool to begin to demonstrate a difference in writing style between various authors of 1 & 2 Nephi. It is effective because—though we look through it with the filter of it being translated from reformed Egyptian into English—we do not have the added refraction of an abridger. As previously mentioned, Mormon simply found Nephi's small plates, and "these things pleasing me..." he added them to the record that would become *The Book of Mormon.*

By chart we will explore the patterns of Nephi's writing style, verses that of Jacob, and finally that of the new voice.

Nephi's pattern of quoting Isaiah is a definable standard, and a pattern which is uniform through 1 & 2 Nephi, except for when Jacob or the new voice is teaching. As an example of this standard, we use 2 Nephi 16 as compared to the King James version of Isaiah 6.

2 Nephi 16	Isaiah 6
1 In the year that king Uzziah died, I saw also the Lord sitting upon a throne, high and lifted up, and his train filled the temple.	1 In the year that king Uzziah died I saw also the Lord sitting upon a throne, high and lifted up, and his train filled the temple.
2 Above it stood the seraphim; each one had six wings; with twain he covered his face, and with twain he covered his feet, and with twain he did fly.	2 Above it stood the seraphims: each one had six wings; with twain he covered his face, and with twain he covered his feet, and with twain he did fly.
3 And one cried unto another, and said: Holy, holy, holy, is the Lord of Hosts; the whole earth is full of his glory.	3 And one cried unto another, and said, Holy, holy, holy, is the Lord of hosts: the whole earth is full of his glory.
4 And the posts of the door moved at the voice of him that cried, and the house was filled with smoke.	4 And the posts of the door moved at the voice of him that cried, and the house was filled with smoke.
5 Then said I: Wo is unto me! for I am undone; because I am a man of unclean lips; and I dwell in the midst of a people of unclean lips; for mine eyes have seen the King, the Lord of Hosts.	5 Then said I, Woe is me! for I am undone; because I am a man of unclean lips, and I dwell in the midst of a people of unclean lips: for mine eyes have seen the King, the Lord of hosts.
6 Then flew one of the seraphim unto me, having a live coal in his hand, which he had taken with the tongs from off the altar;	6 Then flew one of the seraphims unto me, having a live coal in his hand, which he had taken with the tongs from off the altar:
7 And he laid it upon my mouth, and said: Lo, this has touched thy lips; and thine iniquity is taken away, and thy sin purged.	7 And he laid it upon my mouth, and said, Lo, this hath touched thy lips; and thine iniquity is taken away, and thy sin purged.
8 Also I heard the voice of the Lord, saying: Whom shall I send, and who will go for us? Then I said: Here am I; send me.	8 Also I heard the voice of the Lord, saying, Whom shall I send, and who will go for us? Then said I, Here am I; send me.
9 And he said: Go and tell this people—Hear ye indeed, but they understood not; and see ye indeed, but they perceived not.	9 And he said: Go, and tell this people, Hear ye indeed, but understand not; and see ye indeed, but perceive not.

10 Make the heart of this people fat, and make their ears heavy, and shut their eyes—lest they see with their eyes, and hear with their ears, and understand with their heart, and be converted and be healed.	**10** Make the heart of this people fat, and make their ears heavy, and shut their eyes; lest they see with their eyes, and hear with their ears, and understand with their heart, and convert, and be healed.
11 Then said I: Lord, how long? And he said: Until the cities be wasted without inhabitant, and the houses without man, and the land be utterly desolate;	**11** Then said I, Lord, how long? And he answered, Until the cities be wasted without inhabitant, and the houses without man, and the land be utterly desolate,
12 And the Lord have removed men far away, for there shall be a great forsaking in the midst of the land.	**12** And the Lord have removed men far away, and there be a great forsaking in the midst of the land.
13 But yet there shall be a tenth, and they shall return, and shall be eaten, as a teil tree, and as an oak whose substance is in them when they cast their leaves; so the holy seed shall be the substance thereof.	**13** But yet in it shall be a tenth, and it shall return, and shall be eaten: as a teil tree, and as an oak, whose substance is in them, when they cast their leaves: so the holy seed shall be the substance thereof.

We note that *all* Nephi's quoting of Isaiah as included in *The Book of Mormon* follows this pattern. He quotes full chapters without interruption, and then begins commentary and prophesying after. For comparison tables to demonstrate this and all quoting of Isaiah in *The Book of Mormon*, see the appendix of this book.

The Book of Mormon was of course not originally published with chapters and verses as such, but when it was, I imagine that these verses that follow along with King James version of Isaiah were probably the most obvious to delineate. We note that:

1. It begins with the first verse of the Isaiah chapter in reference, according to the King James Version of *the Bible*.

2. There is a one-to-one comparison of the verses between this chapter of *The Book of Mormon,* and words of Isaiah as found in the King James Version of *The Bible,*

3. The entire chapter is quoted.

4. The differences between *The Book of Mormon* version and *The Bible* version of these verses is just a word or two, or a short phrase or two. This is the standard practice with: Nephi: 1 Nephi 20-21, quoting Isaiah 48-49; and 2 Nephi 12-24, quoting Isaiah 2-14; It is true of Abinadi: Mosiah 14, quoting Isaiah 53. It is even true of Jesus Christ: 3 Nephi 22, quoting Isaiah 54.

And—for the most part—Jacob follows this format. 2 Nephi 7-8. (See appendix.) However, there are some differences with the style employed by Jacob as he begins his teachings in 2 Nephi 6 with a sermon of some of the words of the 49ᵗʰ chapter of Isaiah. The first six verses are by way of introduction, and somewhat parallel the intro to Isaiah that Nephi had given in 1 Nephi 19:

First, Nephi's introduction to Isaiah:

> **1 Nephi 19:23-24**
>
> **23** ...I did read unto them that which was written by the prophet Isaiah; for I did liken all scriptures unto us, that it might be for our profit and learning.
>
> **24** Wherefore I spake unto them, saying: Hear ye the words of the prophet, ye who are a remnant of the house of Israel, a branch who have been broken off; hear ye the words of the prophet, which were written unto all the house of Israel, and liken them unto yourselves, that ye may have hope as well as your brethren from whom ye have been broken off; for after this manner has the prophet written.

Then Jacob's introduces us again to Isaiah' writings:

2 Nephi 6:5

5 And now, the words which I shall read are they which Isaiah spake concerning all the house of Israel; wherefore, they may be likened unto you, for ye are of the house of Israel. And there are many things which have been spoken by Isaiah which may be likened unto you, because ye are of the house of Israel.

From the chart below, you will note that Jacob then quotes just two verses from Isaiah 49, and then cuts in with eight verses of explanation and prophesies before continuing on in standard one-to-one format with the balance of that chapter though the next two chapters plus 2 verses.

2 NEPHI 6:6-18	Isaiah 49:22-26
6 And now, these are the words: Thus saith the Lord God: Behold, I will lift up mine hand to the Gentiles, and set up my standard to the people; and they shall bring thy sons in their arms, and thy daughters shall be carried upon their shoulders.	22 Thus saith the Lord God, Behold, I will lift up mine hand to the Gentiles, and set up my standard to the people: and they shall bring thy sons in their arms, and thy daughters shall be carried upon their shoulders.
7 And kings shall be thy nursing fathers, and their queens thy nursing mothers; they shall bow down to thee with their faces towards the earth, and lick up the dust of thy feet; and thou shalt know that I am the Lord; for they shall not be ashamed that wait for me.	23 And kings shall be thy nursing fathers, and their queens thy nursing mothers: they shall bow down to thee with their face toward the earth, and lick up the dust of thy feet; and thou shalt know that I am the Lord: for they shall not be ashamed that wait for me.
8 And now I, Jacob, would speak somewhat concerning these words. For behold, the Lord has shown me that those who were at Jerusalem, from whence we came, have been slain and carried away captive.	

9 Nevertheless, the Lord has shown unto me that they should return again. And he also has shown unto me that the Lord God, the Holy One of Israel, should manifest himself unto them in the flesh; and after he should manifest himself they should scourge him and crucify him, according to the words of the angel who spake it unto me.	
10 And after they have hardened their hearts and stiffened their necks against the Holy One of Israel, behold, the judgements of the Holy One of Israel shall come upon them. And the day cometh that they shall be smitten and afflicted.	
11 Wherefore, after they are driven to and fro, for thus saith the angel, many shall be afflicted in the flesh, and shall not be suffered to perish, because of the prayers of the faithful; they shall be scattered, and smitten, and hated; nevertheless, the Lord will be merciful unto them, that when they shall come to the knowledge of their Redeemer, they shall be gathered together again to the lands of their inheritance.	
12 And blessed are the Gentiles, they of whom the prophet has written; for behold, if it so be that they shall repent and fight not against Zion, and do not unite themselves to that great and abominable church, they shall be saved; for the Lord God will fulfil his covenants which he has made unto his children; and for this cause the prophet has written these things.	

13 Wherefore, they that fight against Zion and the covenant people of the Lord shall lick up the dust of their feet; and the people of the Lord shall not be ashamed. For the people of the Lord are they who wait for him; for they still wait for the coming of the Messiah.	
14 And behold, according to the words of the prophet, the Messiah will set himself again the second time to recover them; wherefore, he will manifest himself unto them in power and great glory, unto the destruction of their enemies, when that day cometh when they shall believe in him; and none will he destroy that believe in him.	
15 And they that believe not in him shall be destroyed, both by fire, and by tempest, and by earthquakes, and by bloodsheds, and by pestilence, and by famine. And they shall know that the Lord is God, the Holy One of Israel.	
16 For shall the prey be taken from the mighty, or the lawful captive delivered?	**24** Shall the prey be taken from the mighty, or the lawful captive delivered?
17 But thus saith the Lord: Even the captives of the mighty shall be taken away, and the prey of the terrible shall be delivered; for the Mighty God shall deliver his covenant people. For thus saith the Lord: I will contend with them that contendeth with thee—	**25** But thus saith the Lord, Even the captives of the mighty shall be taken away, and the prey of the terrible shall be delivered: for I will contend with him that contendeth with thee, and I will save thy children.
18 And I will feed them that oppress thee, with their own flesh; and they shall be drunken with their own blood as with sweet wine; and all flesh shall know that I the Lord am thy Savior and thy Redeemer, the Mighty One of Jacob.	**26** And I will feed them that oppress thee with their own flesh; and they shall be drunken with their own blood, as with sweet wine: and all flesh shall know that I the Lord am thy Saviour and thy Redeemer, the mighty One of Jacob.

Jacob does not quote the entirety of Isaiah 49, probably because Nephi had done so earlier. Be that as it may, he did:

1. Establish that there were additional prophesies that could be obtained by way of the study of the baseline revelations of Isaiah 49 that Nephi had not yet included in the record. This is important for us to realize as we study the words of Isaiah, and perhaps establishes a reason why Jesus Christ quoted Isaiah, when teaching the Nephites. All could receive according to their abilities, level of understanding, and need.

2. Act as an additional testifier to the validity of the teachings of Isaiah and of Nephi.

3. Demonstrate by quoting just a couple of verses and then cutting in to explain and to prophesy that he had a separate and unique voice in his writing.

We will now proceed with an analysis of 2 Nephi 27 as compared to Isaiah 29: Whereas Nephi maintained a strict one-to-one correlation with the verses of Isaiah as found in *The Bible* and then made revelatory statements after. Jacob maintained a strict one-to-one correlation with the verses of Isaiah as found in *The Bible*, but commented sometimes between courses of the one-to-one. In this next section, the voice has a style that is very different from the first two:

2 NEPHI 27: 1-35	Isaiah 29:1-24
	1Woe to Ariel, to Ariel, the city where David dwelt! add ye year to year; let them kill sacrifices.
	2 Yet I will distress Ariel, and there shall be heaviness and sorrow: and it shall be unto me as Ariel.
	3 And I will camp against thee round about, and will lay siege against thee with a mount, and I will raise forts against thee.
	4 And thou shalt be brought down, and shalt speak out of the ground, and thy speech shall be low out of the dust, and thy voice shall be, as of one that hath a familiar spirit, out of the ground, and thy speech shall whisper out of the dust.
	5 Moreover the multitude of thy strangers shall be like small dust, and the multitude of the terrible ones shall be as chaff that passeth away: yea, it shall be at an instant suddenly.
1But, behold, in the last days, or in the days of the Gentiles—yea, behold all the nations of the Gentiles and also the Jews, both those who shall come upon this land and those who shall be upon other lands, yea, even upon all the lands of the earth, behold, they will be drunken with iniquity and all manner of abominations—	
2 And when that day shall come they shall be visited of the Lord of Hosts, with thunder and with earthquake, and with a great noise, and with storm, and with tempest, and with the flame of devouring fire.	6 Thou shalt be visited of the Lord of hosts with thunder, and with earthquake, and great noise, with storm and tempest, and the flame of devouring fire.

3 And all the nations that fight against Zion, and that distress her, shall be as a dream of a night vision; yea, it shall be unto them, even as unto a hungry man which dreameth, and behold he eateth but he awaketh and his soul is empty; or like unto a thirsty man which dreameth, and behold he drinketh but he awaketh and behold he is faint, and his soul hath appetite; yea, even so shall the multitude of all the nations be that fight against Mount Zion.	**7** And the multitude of all the nations that fight against Ariel, even all that fight against her and her munition, and that distress her, shall be as a dream of a night vision. **8** It shall even be as when an hungry man dreameth, and, behold, he eateth; but he awaketh, and his soul is empty: or as when a thirsty man dreameth, and, behold, he drinketh; but he awaketh, and, behold, he is faint, and his soul hath appetite: so shall the multitude of all the nations be, that fight against mount Zion.
4 For behold, all ye that doeth iniquity, stay yourselves and wonder, for ye shall cry out, and cry; yea, ye shall be drunken but not with wine, ye shall stagger but not with strong drink.	**9** Stay yourselves, and wonder; cry ye out, and cry: they are drunken, but not with wine; they stagger, but not with strong drink.
5 For behold, the Lord hath poured out upon you the spirit of deep sleep. For behold, ye have closed your eyes, and ye have rejected the prophets; and your rulers, and the seers hath he covered because of your iniquity.	**10** For the Lord hath poured out upon you the spirit of deep sleep, and hath closed your eyes: the prophets and your rulers, the seers hath he covered.
6 And it shall come to pass that the Lord God shall bring forth unto you the words of a book, and they shall be the words of them which have slumbered.	
7 And behold the book shall be sealed; and in the book shall be a revelation from God, from the beginning of the world to the ending thereof.	

8 Wherefore, because of the things which are sealed up, the things which are sealed shall not be delivered in the day of the wickedness and abominations of the people. Wherefore the book shall be kept from them.	
9 But the book shall be delivered unto a man, and he shall deliver the words of the book, which are the words of those who have slumbered in the dust, and he shall deliver these words unto another;	
10 But the words which are sealed he shall not deliver, neither shall he deliver the book. For the book shall be sealed by the power of God, and the revelation which was sealed shall be kept in the book until the own due time of the Lord, that they may come forth; for behold, they reveal all things from the foundation of the world unto the end thereof.	
11 And the day cometh that the words of the book which were sealed shall be read upon the house tops; and they shall be read by the power of Christ; and all things shall be revealed unto the children of men which ever have been among the children of men, and which ever will be even unto the end of the earth.	
12 Wherefore, at that day when the book shall be delivered unto the man of whom I have spoken, the book shall be hid from the eyes of the world, that the eyes of none shall behold it save it be that three witnesses shall behold it, by the power of God, besides him to whom the book shall be delivered; and they shall testify to the truth of the book and the things therein.	

13 And there is none other which shall view it, save it be a few according to the will of God, to bear testimony of his word unto the children of men; for the Lord God hath said that the words of the faithful should speak as if it were from the dead.	
14 Wherefore, the Lord God will proceed to bring forth the words of the book; and in the mouth of as many witnesses as seemeth him good will he establish his word; and wo be unto him that rejecteth the word of God!	
15 But behold, it shall come to pass that the Lord God shall say unto him to whom he shall deliver the book: Take these words which are not sealed and deliver them to another, that he may show them unto the learned, saying: Read this, I pray thee. And the learned shall say: Bring hither the book, and I will read them. **16** And now, because of the glory of the world and to get gain will they say this, and not for the glory of God. **17**And the man shall say: I cannot bring the book, for it is sealed. **18** Then shall the learned say: I cannot read it.	**11** And the vision of all is become unto you as the words of a book that is sealed, which men deliver to one that is learned, saying, Read this, I pray thee: and he saith, I cannot; for it is sealed:
19 Wherefore it shall come to pass, that the Lord God will deliver again the book and the words thereof to him that is not learned; and the man that is not learned shall say: I am not learned.	**12** And the book is delivered to him that is not learned, saying, Read this, I pray thee: and he saith, I am not learned.

20 Then shall the Lord God say unto him: The learned shall not read them, for they have rejected them, and I am able to do mine own work; wherefore thou shalt read the words which I shall give unto thee.	
21 Touch not the things which are sealed, for I will bring them forth in mine own due time; for I will show unto the children of men that I am able to do mine own work.	
22 Wherefore, when thou hast read the words which I have commanded thee, and obtained the witness which I have promised unto thee, then shalt thou seal up the book again, and hide it up unto me, that I may preserve the words which thou hast not read, until I shall see fit in mine own wisdom to reveal all things unto the children of men.	
23 For behold, I am God; and I am a God of miracles; and I will show unto the world that I am the same yesterday, today, and forever; and I work not among the children of men save it be according to their faith.	
24 And again it shall come to pass that the Lord shall say unto him that shall read the words that shall be delivered him: **25** Forasmuch as this people draw near unto me with their mouth, and with their lips do honor me, but have removed their hearts far from me, and their fear towards me is taught by the precepts of men—	**13** Wherefore the Lord said, Forasmuch as this people draw me with their mouth, and with their lips do honour me, but have removed their heart far from me, and their fear toward me is taught by the precept of men:

26 Therefore, I will proceed to do a marvelous work among this people, yea, a marvelous work and a wonder, for the wisdom of their wise and learned shall perish, and the understanding of their prudent shall be hid.	**14** Therefore, behold, I will proceed to do a marvellous work among this people, even a marvellous work and a wonder: for the wisdom of their wise men shall perish, and the understanding of their prudent men shall be hid.
27 And wo unto them that seek deep to hide their counsel from the Lord! And their works are in the dark; and they say: Who seeth us, and who knoweth us? And they also say: Surely, your turning of things upside down shall be esteemed as the potter's clay. But behold, I will show unto them, saith the Lord of Hosts, that I know all their works. For shall the work say of him that made it, he made me not? Or shall the thing framed say of him that framed it, he had no understanding?	**15** Woe unto them that seek deep to hide their counsel from the Lord, and their works are in the dark, and they say, Who seeth us? and who knoweth us? **16** Surely your turning of things upside down shall be esteemed as the potter's clay: for shall the work say of him that made it, He made me not? or shall the thing framed say of him that framed it, He had no understanding?
28 But behold, saith the Lord of Hosts: I will show unto the children of men that it is yet a very little while and Lebanon shall be turned into a fruitful field; and the fruitful field shall be esteemed as a forest.	**17** Is it not yet a very little while, and Lebanon shall be turned into a fruitful field, and the fruitful field shall be esteemed as a forest?
29 And in that day shall the deaf hear the words of the book, and the eyes of the blind shall see out of obscurity and out of darkness.	**18** And in that day shall the deaf hear the words of the book and the eyes of the blind shall see out of obscurity and out of darkness.
30 And the meek also shall increase, and their joy shall be in the Lord, and the poor among men shall rejoice in the Holy One of Israel.	**19** The meek also shall increase their joy in the Lord, and the poor among men shall rejoice in the Holy One of Israel.
31 For assuredly as the Lord liveth they shall see that the terrible one is brought to naught, and the scorner is consumed, and all that watch for iniquity are cut off;	**20** For the terrible one is brought to nought, and the scorner is consumed, and all that watch for iniquity are cut off:

32 And they that make a man an offender for a word, and lay a snare for him that reproveth in the gate and turn aside the just for a thing of naught.	**21** That make a man an offender for a word, and lay a snare for him that reproveth in the gate and turn aside the just for a thing of nought.
33 Therefore, thus saith the Lord, who redeemed Abraham, concerning the house of Jacob: Jacob shall not now be ashamed, neither shall his face now wax pale.	**22** Therefore thus saith the Lord, who redeemed Abraham, concerning the house of Jacob shall not now be ashamed, neither shall his face now wax pale.
34But when he seeth his children, the work of my hands, in the midst of him, they shall sanctify my name, and sanctify the Holy One of Jacob, and shall fear the God of Israel.	**23** But when he seeth his children, the work of mine hands, in the midst of him, they shall sanctify my name, and sanctify the Holy One of Jacob, and shall fear the God of Israel.
35 They also that erred in spirit shall come to understanding, and they that murmured shall learn doctrine.	**24** They also that erred in spirit shall come to understanding, and they that murmured shall learn doctrine.

1. Contrary to the standard pattern of quoting Isaiah in 1 & 2 Nephi and in *The Book of Mormon* generally, 2 Nephi 27 does *not* begin with the beginning of the chapter of the King James version of Isaiah in reference. This matters because as part of the process, Joseph Smith was certainly using Isaiah as structured in *The Bible*. We note that 2 Nephi 27 omits the first five verses of Isaiah 29. Instead, 2 Nephi 27 starts with revelation. All other chapters in 1 & 2 Nephi that quote Isaiah, do so as the first step in receiving revelation—per the theme of Nephi. But Nephi 27, contrastingly, actually *begins* with some revelation:

> **2 Nephi 27:1**
>
> **1** But, behold, in the last days, or in the days of the Gentiles—yea, behold all the nations of the Gentiles and also the Jews, both those who shall come upon this land

and those who shall be upon other lands, yea, even upon all the lands of the earth, behold, they will be drunken with iniquity and all manner of abominations.

This is certainly unique to 1 & 2 Nephi, but not without precedent from the translator's prospective, since *The Book of Mormon* was translated (after the loss of the Book of Lehi) starting with Mosiah, through Moroni, and then circling back to translate the small plates. (knowhy.bookofmormoncentral.org/knowhy/how-does-the-mosiah-first-translation-sequence-strengthen-faith.) The precedent is from The Savior himself when he taught the Nephites:

3 Nephi 22:26-29

26 And then shall the work of the Father commence at that day, even when this gospel shall be preached among the remnant of this people. Verily I say unto you, at that day shall the work of the Father commence among all the dispersed of my people, yea, even the tribes which have been lost, which the Father hath led away out of Jerusalem.

27 Yea, the work shall commence among all the dispersed of my people, with the Father to prepare the way whereby they may come unto me, that they may call on the Father in my name.

28 Yea, and then shall the work commence, with the Father among all nations in preparing the way whereby his people may be gathered home to the land of their inheritance.

29 And they shall go out from all nations; and they shall not go out in haste, nor go by flight, for I will go before them, saith the Father, and I will be their rearward.

253

Which leads right into the Lord quoting Isaiah—who was quoting the Lord.

> **3 Nephi 22:1-3 (compare Isaiah 22:1-3)**
>
> **1** And then shall that which is written come to pass: Sing, O barren, thou that didst not bear; break forth into singing, and cry aloud, thou that didst not travail with child; for more are the children of the desolate than the children of the married wife, saith the Lord.
>
> **2** Enlarge the place of thy tent, and let them stretch forth the curtains of thy habitations; spare not, lengthen thy cords and strengthen thy stakes;
>
> **3** For thou shalt break forth on the right hand and on the left, and thy seed shall inherit the Gentiles and make the desolate cities to be inhabited.

2. Contrary to the standard pattern of quoting Isaiah in 1 & 2 Nephi and in *The Book of Mormon* generally, there is *not* a one-to-one comparison of the verses between this chapter and words of Isaiah as found in the King James version of *The Bible*.

   a. 2 Nephi 27 omits Isaiah 29:1-5;

   b. 2 Nephi 27:6-14,—nine verses—does not directly correspond with any verses in Isaiah 29. Instead it is new revelation inserted between cited verses.

   c. 2 Nephi 27:15-18, four verses, corresponds to just one verse: Isaiah 29:11.

   d. 2 Nephi 27: 20-23, four verses, does not directly correspond with any verses in Isaiah 29.

e. 2 Nephi 27:25-35 correspond with Isaiah 13-24, but it should be noted that 2 Nephi 27:27 corresponds with two verses: Isaiah 29:15-16

3. The segue. There is an interesting little "between" verse unique to this new voice, the likes of which Nephi never needed to use:

> **2 Nephi 27:24**
>
> 24 And again it shall come to pass that the Lord shall say unto him that shall read the words that shall be delivered him:

This verse appears to be an intentional segue from the end of a section of specific revelation, back to a one-to-one verse correspondence to King James version Isaiah from this point to the end of the chapter.

But it is even more than that: It appears as an identifier to Joseph Smith that this revelation is for him as the first prophet and leader of the church in this dispensation; that *he* was given specific insight and understanding of the world he lived in and the role he was to play in it. This was as plain as words can make it, nothing lost in translation, no detail lost in passing through Nephi, who may have seen, but did not live in rural New York in the early 1900's. For Joseph Smith, this was not old text. The first part of the revelation helped clarify the troubles that he went through with the loss of the 116 pages of manuscript and that clarity prepared him for the second section of this revelation, which was as the present and ongoing word of God for him at that time.

Whatever Joseph Smith was before, this confirmed him a Prophet.

And what about the next two chapters? Of course he should prophesy, per the pattern set by Nephi.

4. The second half of 2 Nephi 27.

There are phrase changes in many of the verses, indicating a style of specificity that is not found in the standard pattern of quoting Isaiah in *The Book of Mormon*. We take some examples beginning at the segue point 2 Nephi 27:25 to the end of that chapter, where it is written in a (mostly) verse-to-verse correspondence to King James version Isaiah. Namely:

a. It omits the more simple phrase "Wherefore the Lord said" in Isaiah 29:13;

b. It adds "But behold, I will show unto them, saith the Lord of Hosts, that I know all their works." to Isaiah 29:16;

c. It adds "But behold, saith the Lord of Hosts:" to Isaiah 29:17;

d. It adds "assuredly as the Lord liveth they shall see that" to Isaiah 29:20.

e. It also includes a few changes that are arguably more minor, and certainly more typical of the slight differences between *The Book of Mormon* translation and the King James version of Isaiah.

All of which seem to indicate that though it is all excellent instruction, the new revelation based upon Isaiah 29 as included in 2 Nephi 27 is essentially over by verse 24. However the *voice of a greater meticulousness* pervades until the end of this chapter. For example, we return to:

Isaiah 6:9-10

9 And he said, Go, and tell this people, Hear ye indeed, but understand not; and see ye indeed, but perceive not.

10 Make the heart of this people fat, and make their ears heavy, and shut their eyes; lest they see with their eyes, and hear with their ears, and understand with their heart, and convert, and be healed.

Which Nephi translates as:

2 Nephi 16:9-10

9 And he said: Go and tell this people—Hear ye indeed, but they understood not; and see ye indeed, but they perceived not.

10 Make the heart of this people fat, and make their ears heavy, and shut their eyes—lest they see with their eyes, and hear with their ears, and understand with their heart, and be converted and be healed.

As opposed to the new voice:

Isaiah 29:10

10 For the Lord hath poured out upon you the spirit of deep sleep, and hath closed your eyes: the prophets and your rulers, the seers hath he covered.

Which is translated as:

> **2 Nephi 27: 5**
>
> **5** For behold, the Lord hath poured out upon you the spirit of deep sleep. *For behold, ye have* closed your eyes, *and ye have rejected* the prophets; and your rulers, and the seers hath he covered because of your iniquity.

Another example of this "meticulousness" can be found in a more general comparison from these same two chapters—2 Nephi 16 and 2 Nephi 27. If it were the same writer, would not the writer who added phrases like "the Lord of Hosts" several times in the latter verse-to-verse patterned portion of 2 Nephi 27 have like-wise used them in describing the words of the Lord when seen seated on his throne in his court in his temple? Instead it is a couple of simple "he said" 's.

> **2 Nephi 16:9-11**
>
> **9** And *he said*: Go and tell this people—Hear ye indeed, but they understood not; and see ye indeed, but they perceived not.
>
> **10** Make the heart of this people fat, and make their ears heavy, and shut their eyes—lest they see with their eyes, and hear with their ears, and understand with their heart, and be converted and be healed.
>
> **11** Then said I: Lord, how long? And *he said*: Until the cities be wasted without inhabitant, and the houses without man, and the land be utterly desolate;

These differences signal a change in style, which suggests that there is a new voice in this section of the scriptures.

Item 5: *Explore various evidence that these chapters were written in a new voice.* There are enough and significant differences between these chapters and the other chapters of 2 Nephi that quote and elucidate the revelations of Isaiah, to indicate that 2 Nephi chapters 27-29 were written by another person. Why are there differences? Because God speaks to a person according to his own language.

> **2 Nephi 31:3**
>
> **3** For my soul delighteth in plainness; for after this manner doth the Lord God work among the children of men. For the Lord God giveth light unto the understanding; for he speaketh unto men according to their language, unto their understanding.

This means that for Joseph Smith, he perceived the concepts in the revelations in a format that was according to his understanding, which we will demonstrate was different than did Nephi.

Evidence #5.1: Unique or missing words and phrases: "I Nephi". The phrase "I Nephi" is used eighty-five times in the other chapters of 1 & 2 Nephi, but it is never used in the 2 Nephi 27-29. In fact, the name Nephi, is only used once in these chapters, and then not in the first person:

> **2 Nephi 29:2**
>
> **2** And also, that I may remember the promises which I have made unto thee, Nephi, and also unto thy father, that I would remember your seed; and that the words of your seed should proceed forth out of my mouth unto your seed; and my words shall hiss forth unto the ends of the earth, for a standard unto my people, which are of the house of Israel;

The name of Nephi is only invoked once in these three chapters, and in that one instance the Lord is speaking to him about blessing his posterity at some distant generation with the opportunity to accept the gospel.

Evidence #5.1.2: Whereas Nephi had at both previous opportunities immediately identified himself after a quote from Isaiah and as he commenced his commentary and prophesying:

> **1 Nephi 22:1** *(immediately follows two chapters of Isaiah)*
>
> 1 And now it came to pass that after I, Nephi, had read these things which were engraven upon the plates of brass, my brethren came unto me and said unto me: What meaneth these things which ye have read? Behold, are they to be understood according to things which are spiritual, which shall come to pass according to the spirit and not the flesh?

And:

> **2 Nephi 25:1** *(immediately follows thirteen chapters of Isaiah)*
>
> 1 Now *I, Nephi,* do speak somewhat concerning the words which I have written, which have been spoken by the mouth of Isaiah. For behold, Isaiah spake many things which were hard for many of my people to understand; for they know not concerning the manner of prophesying among the Jews.

This does not happen in 2 Nephi 28. In fact 2 Nephi chapters 27-28 do not contain the name Nephi. Nephi *is* mentioned once in chapter 29, but as stated above, the name is not used in the first-person.

Evidence #5.1.3: However, "I, Nephi," is found in the very first verse after this anomaly:

> **2 Nephi 30:1**
>
> 1 And now behold, my beloved brethren, I would speak
> unto you; for I, Nephi, would …

This indicates that Nephi is identified again as the writer, and points to there being a different voice for those previous three chapters.

Evidence #5.2: Unique or missing words and phrases: The term "Nephite" used in this section, but not elsewhere in 1 & 2 Nephi. Actually, it appears to be a termed coined by Jacob:

> **Jacob 1:12-14**
>
> 12 And it came to pass that Nephi died.
>
> 13 Now the people which were not Lamanites were Nephites; nevertheless, they were called Nephites, Jacobites, Josephites, Zoramites, Lamanites, Lemuelites, and Ishmaelites.
>
> 14 But I, Jacob, shall not hereafter distinguish them by these names, but I shall call them Lamanites that seek to destroy the people of Nephi, and those who are friendly to Nephi I shall call Nephites, or the people of Nephi, according to the reigns of the kings.

However, it is used in this anomalous section:

> **2 Nephi 29:12-13**
>
> 12 For behold, I shall speak unto the Jews and they shall write it; and I shall also speak unto the Nephites and they shall write it; and I shall also speak unto the other tribes of the house of Israel, which I have led away, and they shall write it; and I shall also speak unto all nations of the earth and they shall write it.

> **13** And it shall come to pass that the Jews shall have the words of the Nephites, and the Nephites shall have the words of the Jews; and the Nephites and the Jews shall have the words of the lost tribes of Israel; and the lost tribes of Israel shall have the words of the Nephites and the Jews.

This points to a new voice, and implies a later voice, a voice that was already familiar with the term "Nephite" for these three chapters. I refer you to the Mosiah-first translation order as explained earlier.

Evidence #5.3: Unique or missing words and phrases: The term "Bible" is used in this section, but not elsewhere in 1 & 2 Nephi:

> **2 Nephi 29:6**
>
> **6** Thou fool, that shall say: A Bible, we have got a Bible, and we need no more Bible. Have ye obtained a Bible save it were by the Jews?

In fact, in the vision that Nephi has that includes the coming forth of the Bible, he refers to it in more generic terms:

> **1 Nephi 13: 20-24**
>
> **20** And it came to pass that I, Nephi, beheld that they did prosper in the land; and I beheld a book, and it was carried forth among them.
>
> **21** And the angel said unto me: Knowest thou the meaning of the book?
>
> **22** And I said unto him: I know not.
>
> **23** And he said: Behold it proceedeth out of the mouth of a Jew. And I, Nephi, beheld it; and he said unto me: The book that thou beholdest is a record of the Jews, which

contains the covenants of the Lord, which he hath made unto the house of Israel; and it also containeth many of the prophecies of the holy prophets; and it is a record like unto the engravings which are upon the plates of brass, save there are not so many; nevertheless, they contain the covenants of the Lord, which he hath made unto the house of Israel; wherefore, they are of great worth unto the Gentiles.

24 And the angel of the Lord said unto me: Thou hast beheld that the book proceeded forth from the mouth of a Jew; and when it proceeded forth from the mouth of a Jew it contained the fulness of the gospel of the Lord, of whom the twelve apostles bear record; and they bear record according to the truth which is in the Lamb of God.

This points to a new voice for these three chapters.

Evidence #5.4: 2 Nephi 27 excludes any reference about Jerusalem. Isaiah 29, upon which 2 Nephi 27 is based, mentions Jerusalem five times in the first seven verses. And one would suppose that had Nephi written it, he would not have omitted all of the verses that mentioned his home town.

Isaiah 29:1-7

1 Woe to Ariel, to Ariel, the city where David dwelt! add ye year to year; let them kill sacrifices.

2 Yet I will distress Ariel, and there shall be heaviness and sorrow: and it shall be unto me as Ariel.

3 And I will camp against thee round about, and will lay siege against thee with a mount, and I will raise forts against thee.

4 And thou shalt be brought down, and shalt speak out of the ground, and thy speech shall be low out of the dust,

and thy voice shall be, as of one that hath a familiar spirit, out of the ground, and thy speech shall whisper out of the dust.

5 Moreover the multitude of thy strangers shall be like small dust, and the multitude of the terrible ones shall be as chaff that passeth away: yea, it shall be at an instant suddenly.

6 Thou shalt be visited of the Lord of hosts with thunder, and with earthquake, and great noise, with storm and tempest, and the flame of devouring fire.

7 And the multitude of all the nations that fight against Ariel, even all that fight against her and her munition, and that distress her, shall be as a dream of a night vision.

(Barnes Notes on the Bible, biblehub.com)

"To Ariel- There can be no doubt that Jerusalem is here intended."

(Benson Commentary, biblehub.com)

"Isaiah 29:1 'Wo to Ariel'... 'That Jerusalem is here called by this name,' says Bishop Lowth, 'is very certain.'"

It is very unlikely that Nephi—who had lived at Jerusalem, who was from Jerusalem, who went back to Jerusalem for the brass plates in peril of his life, who returned again to Jerusalem for Ishmael's family, who prophesied the destruction of Jerusalem, who prophesied the re-building and re-inhabitation of Jerusalem would opt to exclude these verses, or to change one of them to read "Zion" instead. This points to someone other than Nephi writing these chapters.

Evidence #5.4.2: Nowhere else in Nephi's pattern of quoting Isaiah, does he ever omit so many verses, and nowhere else does he not start his quote with the first verse of a chapter as found in KJV Isaiah. One way to demonstrate this is to chart all of Nephi's quoting of Isaiah in columnar format with the KJV Isaiah chapters listed in the second column corresponding verse by verse—which can be found in the appendix of this book. This points to a new voice in these three chapters.

Evidence #5.5: Prospective of one in the current dispensation: In 2 Nephi 29, The writer refers to the Jews as "mine *ancient* covenant people".

> **2 Nephi 29:4**
>
> 4 But thus saith the Lord God: O fools, they shall have a Bible; and it shall proceed forth from the Jews, *mine ancient covenant people*. And what thank they the Jews for the Bible which they receive from them? Yea, what do the Gentiles mean? Do they remember the travails, and the labors, and the pains of the Jews, and their diligence unto me, in bringing forth salvation unto the Gentiles?

However, elsewhere Nephi never refers to the Jews as "ancient." Why not?

> **Old Testament Student Manual Kings-Malachi. The Church of Jesus Christ of Latter-day Saints.**
>
> In 721 B.C. Assyria swept out of the north, captured the Northern Kingdom of Israel, and took the ten tribes into captivity. From there they became lost to history.

The reason that the Jews were not considered the "ancient covenant people" by Nephi is that the ancient covenant people to Nephi were all of Israel, the lost ten tribes only becoming lost some 121 years before Nephi and his father's family left Jerusalem.

Elsewhere—and even nearly a millennium later—the Jews are recognized as simply "the covenant people" by the next editor:

> **Mormon 3:21**
>
> **21** And also that ye may believe the gospel of Jesus Christ, which ye shall have among you; and also that the Jews, *the covenant people* of the Lord, shall have other witness besides him whom they saw and heard, that Jesus, whom they slew, was the very Christ and the very God.

This implies that "ancient" is used in 2 Nephi 29:4-5 as an adjective that modifies "people", not "covenant". It also implies a new, later voice. They were not ancient in Nephi's time, and not even that ancient in Mormon's time as they were in the time of Joseph Smith.

Evidence #5.6: Perspective: Speaking for God—in the first person. Elsewhere, Nephi never writes speaking for God in the first person. Some of the quotes that Nephi uses do so, but not Nephi himself. Even during his closing remarks when Nephi hears the voice of the Father and also of the Son, Nephi does not speak/write in their respective voices, but still only reports from his perspective:

> **2 Nephi 31:11-12, 14-15**
>
> **11** And the Father said: ...
>
> **12** And also, the voice of the Son came unto me, saying: ....
>
> **14** But, behold, my beloved brethren, thus came the voice of the Son unto me, saying:...

> **15** And I heard a voice from the Father, saying:...

Even when Nephi says: "Thus saith the Lord", he is quoting the Lord, and not speaking in the first person:

> **2 Nephi 26:17-18**
>
> **17** *For thus saith the Lord God*: They shall write the things which shall be done among them, and they shall be written and sealed up in a book, and those who have dwindled in unbelief shall not have them, for they seek to destroy the things of God.
>
> **18** Wherefore, as those who have been destroyed have been destroyed speedily; and the multitude of their terrible ones shall be as chaff that passeth away—yea, *thus saith the Lord God*: It shall be at an instant, suddenly...

It is not simply a matter of respect, but it appears to be more of a literary style, or perhaps an additional meaning that we will explore soon.

The style is different in the section in question. 2 Nephi 29 is entirely written as the Lord speaking in the first person. Note the copious use of the pronoun "I", and the possessives "my" and "mine" in referring to the Lord's people.

> **2 Nephi 29: 1-14**
>
> **1** But behold, there shall be many—at that day when I shall proceed to do a marvelous work among them, that *I* may remember my covenants which *I* have made unto the children of men, that *I* may set my hand again the second time to recover my people, which are of the house of Israel;

2And also, that *I* may remember the promises which *I* have made unto thee, Nephi, and also unto thy father, that *I* would remember your seed; and that the words of your seed should proceed forth out of *my* mouth unto your seed; and *my* words shall hiss forth unto the ends of the earth, for a standard unto my people, which are of the house of Israel;

3 And because my words shall hiss forth—many of the Gentiles shall say: A Bible! A Bible! We have got a Bible, and there cannot be any more Bible.

4 But thus saith the Lord God: O fools, they shall have a Bible; and it shall proceed forth from the Jews, *mine* ancient covenant people. And what thank they the Jews for the Bible which they receive from them? Yea, what do the Gentiles mean? Do they remember the travails, and the labors, and the pains of the Jews, and their diligence unto *me*, in bringing forth salvation unto the Gentiles?

5 O ye Gentiles, have ye remembered the Jews, *mine* ancient covenant people? Nay; but ye have cursed them, and have hated them, and have not sought to recover them. But behold, *I* will return all these things upon your own heads; for *I* the Lord have not forgotten *my* people.

6 Thou fool, that shall say: A Bible, we have got a Bible, and we need no more Bible. Have ye obtained a Bible save it were by the Jews?

7 Know ye not that there are more nations than one? Know ye not that *I*, the Lord your God, have created all men, and that *I* remember those who are upon the isles of the sea; and that *I* rule in the heavens above and in the earth beneath; and *I* bring forth *my* word unto the children of men, yea, even upon all the nations of the earth?

8 Wherefore murmur ye, because that ye shall receive more of *my* word? Know ye not that the testimony of two nations

is a witness unto you that *I* am God, that *I* remember one nation like unto another? Wherefore, *I* speak the same words unto one nation like unto another. And when the two nations shall run together the testimony of the two nations shall run together also.

9 And *I* do this that *I* may prove unto many that *I* am the same yesterday, today, and forever; and that *I* speak forth *my* words according to mine own pleasure. And because that I have spoken one word ye need not suppose that I cannot speak another; for *my* work is not yet finished; neither shall it be until the end of man, neither from that time henceforth and forever.

10 Wherefore, because that ye have a Bible ye need not suppose that it contains all *my* words; neither need ye suppose that *I* have not caused more to be written.

11 For *I* command all men, both in the east and in the west, and in the north, and in the south, and in the islands of the sea, that they shall write the words which *I* speak unto them; for out of the books which shall be written *I* will judge the world, every man according to their works, according to that which is written.

12 For behold, *I* shall speak unto the Jews and they shall write it; and *I* shall also speak unto the Nephites and they shall write it; and *I* shall also speak unto the other tribes of the house of Israel, which *I* have led away, and they shall write it; and *I* shall also speak unto all nations of the earth and they shall write it.

13 And it shall come to pass that the Jews shall have the words of the Nephites, and the Nephites shall have the words of the Jews; and the Nephites and the Jews shall have the words of the lost tribes of Israel; and the lost tribes of Israel shall have the words of the Nephites and the Jews.

> **14** And it shall come to pass that *my* people, which are of the house of Israel, shall be gathered home unto the lands of their possessions; and *my* word also shall be gathered in one. And *I* will show unto them that fight against *my* word and against *my* people, who are of the house of Israel, that *I* am God, and that *I* covenanted with Abraham that *I* would remember his seed forever.

This drastic change in style suggests that there is a new voice in these three chapters.

Evidence #5.7: Literary style: Rhetorical questions. Simply put: They are not typical of Nephi's writing style, except when he is speaking within himself in what we refer to as "The Psalm of Nephi"—2 Nephi 4. Nephi only uses rhetorical questions again in his closing remarks. They are however, used in abundance in 2 Nephi 29:

> **2 Nephi 29: 4-8**
>
> **4** *...And what thank they the Jews for the Bible which they receive from them? Yea, what do the Gentiles mean? Do they remember the travails, and the labors, and the pains of the Jews, and their diligence unto me, in bringing forth salvation unto the Gentiles?*
>
> **5** *O ye Gentiles, have ye remembered the Jews, mine ancient covenant people?* Nay; but ye have cursed them, and have hated them, and have not sought to recover them. But behold, I will return all these things upon your own heads; for I the Lord have not forgotten my people.
>
> **6** Thou fool, that shall say: A Bible, we have got a Bible, and we need no more Bible. *Have ye obtained a Bible save it were by the Jews?*

> **7** *Know ye not that there are more nations than one? Know ye not that I, the Lord your God, have created all men, and that I remember those who are upon the isles of the sea; and that I rule in the heavens above and in the earth beneath; and I bring forth my word unto the children of men, yea, even upon all the nations of the earth?*
>
> **8** *Wherefore murmur ye, because that ye shall receive more of my word? Know ye not that the testimony of two nations is a witness unto you that I am God, that I remember one nation like unto another?*

The use of so many rhetorical questions suggests a new voice in these chapters.

We note that Evidence #6 and Evidence #7 combined are consistent with:

> **2 Nephi 31:3**
>
> **3** ... for after this manner doth the Lord God work among the children of men. For the Lord God giveth light unto the understanding; for he speaketh unto men according to their language, unto their understanding.

It appears by the style and language of transmission, that the young Joseph Smith discerned much of the new revelation in rhetorical questions, and with words from God spoken in the first-person, etc., not unlike early nineteenth century (perhaps Methodist?) preachers, who would have influenced the language of a child of the frontier, especially pertaining to religious matters.

> **Joseph Smith—History 1:5,8**
>
> **5** Some time in the second year after our removal to Manchester, there was in the place where we lived

an unusual excitement on the subject of religion. It commenced with the Methodists, but soon became general among all the sects in that region of country. Indeed, the whole district of country seemed affected by it, and great multitudes united themselves to the different religious parties, which created no small stir and division amongst the people, some crying, Lo, here!" and others, "Lo, there!" Some were contending for the Methodist faith, some for the Presbyterian, and some for the Baptist.

8 During this time of great excitement my mind was called up to serious reflection and great uneasiness; but though my feelings were deep and often poignant, still I kept myself aloof from all these parties, though I attended their several meetings as often as occasion would permit. In process of time my mind became somewhat partial to the Methodist sect, and I felt some desire to be united with them; but so great were the confusion and strife among the different denominations, that it was impossible for a person young as I was, and so unacquainted with men and things, to come to any certain conclusion who was right and who was wrong.

We should not be surprised by this writing style. This points not only to a different voice, but more directly to Joseph Smith.

Item 6: *Examine the one verse in this section that uniquely points to Nephi, and why it fits with the way that Joseph Smith conveyed this revelation in the text.* In other words I would like to demonstrate that the "fly" in the soup is actually part of the soup.

There is one verse in this 3-chapter section that points to the voice of Nephi:

2 Nephi 28:2

2 And the things which shall be written out of the book shall be of great worth unto the children of men, and especially unto our seed, which is a remnant of the house of Israel.

Our seed. The question then is this: Is it unheard of that a prophet expresses revelation as if through the voice of another? We need not go far to find the answer in the form of an example. In the following excerpt, Nephi is quoting Isaiah, who is conveying revelation at this time in the voice of either fir trees, or (more likely) an ethereal "they". (i.e. "you know what *they* say...") This voice in turn is quoting the king of Babylon/Lucifer.

2 Nephi 14: 4, 8, 10-14

4 And it shall come to pass in that day, that thou shalt take up this against the king of Babylon, and say: How hath the oppressor ceased, the golden city ceased!

8 Yea, the fir trees rejoice at thee, and also the cedars of Lebanon, saying: Since thou art laid down no feller is come up against us.

10 All they shall speak and say unto thee: Art thou also become weak as we? Art thou become like unto us?

11 Thy pomp is brought down to the grave; the noise of thy viols is not heard; the worm is spread under thee, and the worms cover thee.

12 How art thou fallen from heaven, O Lucifer, son of the morning! Art thou cut down to the ground, which did weaken the nations!

13 For thou hast said in thy heart: I will ascend into heaven, I will exalt my throne above the stars of God; I will sit also upon the mount of the congregation, in the sides of the north;

14 I will ascend above the heights of the clouds; I will be like the Most High.

Truly this is no more complex than some of our favorite hymns: Eliza R. Snow penned the words to #191 "Behold the Great Redeemer Die". In it the first three verses are told from a third-person perspective at the time of the crucifixion. The fourth verse from Christ's perspective in the Garden of Gethsemane, (obviously prior to the crucifixion) and ends as he dies on the cross. Verse 5 returns to the original third-person onsite perspective, and verse 6 is told from the view of us now, singing in the church pews and preparing to partake of the sacrament.

Hymns of the Church of Jesus Christ of Latter-day Saints, 1985. Hymn 191, "Behold the Great Redeemer Die"

1 Behold the great Redeemer die, A broken law to satisfy.

He dies a sacrifice for sin, that man may live and glory win.

2 While guilty men his pains deride, they pierce his hands and feet and side;

And with insulting scoffs and scorns, They crown his head with plaited thorns.

3 Although in agony he hung, No murmuring word escaped his tongue.

His high commission to fulfill, He magnified his Father's will.

4 "Father, from me remove this cup. Yet, if thou wilt, I'll drink it up.

I've done the work thou gavest me, Receive my spirit unto thee.

5 He died, and at the awful sight the sun in shame withdrew its light!

Earth trembled, and all nature sighed In dread response, "A God has died!"

6 He lives—he lives. We humble now Around these sacred symbols bow And seek, as saints of latter days, To do his will and live his praise.

We seem to have more liberal rules to writers of sacred hymn lyrics. Indeed we can learn a lot from Isaiah if we were to just consider his writings as hymns—perhaps set to music such that they could be taught to and memorized by a largely illiterate population in the old kingdoms of the Holy Land.

Secondarily, this verse:

2 Nephi 28:2

2 And the things which shall be written out of the book shall be of great worth unto the children of men, and especially unto our seed, which is a remnant of the house of Israel.

—is actually a short version of a message posted two chapters later, which segment begins with identifying the writer as Nephi (2 Nephi 30:1)

2 Nephi 30:3-6

3 ...For after the book of which I have spoken shall come forth, and be written unto the Gentiles, and sealed up again unto the Lord, there shall be many which shall believe the words which are written; and they shall carry them forth unto the remnant of our seed.

4 And then shall the remnant of our seed know concerning us, how that we came out from Jerusalem, and that they are descendants of the Jews.

5 And the gospel of Jesus Christ shall be declared among them; wherefore, they shall be restored unto the knowledge of their fathers, and also to the knowledge of Jesus Christ, which was had among their fathers.

6 And then shall they rejoice; for they shall know that it is a blessing unto them from the hand of God; and their scales of darkness shall begin to fall from their eyes; and many generations shall not pass away among them, save they shall be a pure and a delightsome people.

It is noteworthy that this message is listed twice, but that the first time was not via the words of Isaiah. This also begs the question: Is the shorter version a preview or is it a synopsis? In other words, did the prophet receive 2 Nephi 27-29 after he had translated 2 Nephi 30?

Item 7: Eliminate possible writers and identify the actual writer of this section of scripture.

These differences introduce the possibility of another voice in the record. There are only four who could have affected the record:

1. Nephi himself.

2. Jacob, younger brother of Nephi, next prophet and heir-apparent of the small plates of Nephi.

3. Mormon, abridger of *The Book of Mormon.*

4. Joseph Smith, translator of *The Book of Mormon.*

Nephi: Based on all of the data-points submitted above demonstrating the differences between Nephi's voice and the new voice, we can conclude that the name of Nephi can be struck from this list.

Jacob: Since these small plates would be transferred from Nephi to Jacob, and since Jacob had readily identified himself at the beginning of his writings

> **2 Nephi 6:1-3**
>
> 1 The words of Jacob, the brother of Nephi, which he spake unto the people of Nephi:
>
> 2 Behold, my beloved brethren, I, Jacob, having been called of God, and ordained after the manner of his holy order, and having been consecrated by my brother Nephi, unto whom ye look as a king or a protector, and on whom ye depend for safety, behold ye know that I have spoken unto you exceedingly many things.
>
> 3 Nevertheless, I speak unto you again...

and

> **Jacob 1:1-2**
>
> 1 For behold, it came to pass that fifty and five years had passed away from the time that Lehi left Jerusalem; wherefore, Nephi gave me, Jacob, a commandment concerning the small plates, upon which these things are engraven.

> **2** And he gave me, Jacob, a commandment that I should write upon these plates a few of the things which I considered to be most precious...

And since Nephi tells us when Jacob has ended his turn at writing, and states that Jacob will not write again in 2 Nephi:

> **2 Nephi 11:1**
>
> **1** And now, Jacob spake many more things to my people at that time; nevertheless *only these things* have I caused to be written, for the things which I have written sufficeth me.

We can safely exclude Jacob.

Mormon: Mormon similarly identifies himself:

> **Words of Mormon 1:1**
>
> **1**And now I, Mormon, being about to deliver up the record which I have been making into the hands of my son Moroni, behold I have witnessed almost all the destruction of my people, the Nephites.
>
> **3 Nephi 28:24**
>
> **24** And now I, Mormon, make an end of speaking concerning these things for a time.

And there is the identifier that is located several verses after his third-person narrative of Christ teaching the Nephites had morphed into Mormon's own statements.

> **4 Nephi 1: 23**
>
> 23 And now I, Mormon, would that ye should know that the people had multiplied, insomuch that they were spread upon all the face of the land, and that they had become exceedingly rich, because of their prosperity in Christ.
>
> **Mormon 1:1**
>
> 1 And now I, Mormon, make a record of the things which I have both seen and heard, and call it The Book of Mormon.

We note that there are many instances in *The Book of Mormon* where there are side editorials that are somewhat separate from the account and also written in a way that is often describing the principle by speaking of those in the narrative in the third person. For example:

> **Ether 14:25**
>
> 25*And thus we see* that the Lord did visit them in the fulness of his wrath, and their wickedness and abominations had prepared a way for their everlasting destruction.

For this one verse of additional declaration inserted into the narrative, there are three possible authors:

The first possibility is that Ether was inspired by God to include it; that Moroni, the editor was equally inspired to not exclude it; and that Joseph Smith received it through the revelatory-translation process.

The second possibility is that Moroni, who was the editor in this case, was inspired by God to add it; and that Joseph Smith received it through the revelatory-translation process. (For this particular example, this is the one that I am leaning toward.)

The third possibility is that Joseph Smith received it through the revelatory-translation process and added it at that later stage in the process.

From this we learn two things: These three possibilities, the author at the time of the narrative, the editor, and the translator are all in play for credit for most of the many, smaller unattributed side-observations. And that because of the difficulty in identifying the originally inspired, these extra declarations are of little worth in determining the likelihood of Mormon or Joseph Smith in writing this three-chapter anomaly.

Therefore, finding no absolute evidence that Mormon was the author of all of the unattributed side comments, and with the implication that Mormon copied the small plates without editing nor abridging them (Words of Mormon 1:3-7); and based upon the strength of the previous evidence that Mormon habitually identifies himself in his commentary—we can remove his name from consideration.

And then there was one: Joseph Smith, the seer.

Knowing that he was also a special witness of Jesus Christ, and understanding from Nephi's prophesy that "God sendeth more witnesses," we can rest assured that Joseph Smith asked and received confirmation that he was to add his testimony to the existing work.

+ + + +

A few concluding points:

First: A macro-view study of the small plates of Nephi allows us to see Nephi's theme with sufficient clarity to easily identify and then appreciably analyze the indicators of this anomaly as if they were the echoing ripples from a stone tossed into an otherwise calm pond. Joseph Smith included his testimony, just as he was instructed.

Nephi's theme includes teaching us how to receive revelation through the study and prayerful contemplation of Isaiah's writings. Even when Isaiah wrote of historical events of his time period (some 150 years prior) Nephi could "liken them" to himself and his people, and thereby receive revelation pertaining to his people.

In this dispensation, this lesson was first taught to and learned by the prophet Joseph Smith, during the translation process.

> ### Doctrine & Covenants 9: 7-8
>
> 7 Behold, you have not understood; you have supposed that I would give it unto you, when you took no thought save it was to ask me.
>
> 8 But, behold, I say unto you, that you must study it out in your mind; then you must ask me if it be right, and if it is right I will cause that your bosom shall burn within you; therefore, you shall feel that it is right.

This illustrates the revelatory nature of translation through the use of the Urim and Thummim, and informed Oliver Cowdery personally how he would perceive the witness of the spirit. As Oliver learned per *Doctrine and Covenants* sections 8 and 9, these were not merely "peep-stones" which could automate translation and might be connected to a computer/mechanical device for recording, but that they instead were more of a facilitator of revelation, and if not prepared to receive revelation he would not be able to effectively use them. As we learn from Ammon:

> **Mosiah: 8:13, 15-16**
>
> **13** Now Ammon said unto him: I can assuredly tell thee, O king, of a man that can translate the records; for he has wherewith that he can look, and translate all records that are of ancient date; and it is a gift from God. And the things are called interpreters, and no man can look in them except he be commanded, lest he should look for that he ought not and he should perish. And whosoever is commanded to look in them, the same is called seer...
>
> **15** And the king said that a seer is greater than a prophet.
>
> **16** And Ammon said that *a seer is a revelator and a prophet also*;

It appears that Oliver Cowdery had not understood this new concept and had attempted to act as a seer without acting as a revelator and a prophet. We understand that the studying of it out in one's mind allows deity to confirm the gift of knowledge without inhibiting agency. Since the source of *The Book of Mormon* as given to Joseph Smith is perhaps at least as much revelation as it is hieroglyphics written on golden plates, it would not be much of a stretch that this small section of the work was not directed through Nephi's glyphs.

This also offers insight into the ancient portions of *The Pearl of Great Price*.

This data points to this section of scripture being a revelation received by Joseph Smith apart from what was etched onto the golden plates, and that it was received and written in the pattern of the theme of Nephi. And it also speaks to the method of translation, or at least, how much the gift of translation relies on the gift of revelation.

Secondly: Joseph Smith was instructed by and prophesied to by the prophet Moroni. (Joseph-Smith History 1:30-49) We note that the process of prophesying used by Moroni to Joseph Smith on this occasion was similar to Nephi's theme, in that Moroni quoted prophesies attributed to other prophets—Malachi, Isaiah, Moses and Joel—creating a foundation of additional witness and then adding his prophesies to theirs. Important to this point is that these revelations via Moroni included that Joseph Smith was called to be a seer. (Joseph Smith History 1:35, 42).

Next, per the Mosiah-first order of the translation of *The Book of Mormon* as previously described, Joseph Smith was taught by Ammon that a seer—which Joseph Smith was called by prophesy to be, and which he was serving as even in this translation process—"is a revelator and a prophet also." (Mosiah 8:16) Later, nearing the end of the translation process of *The Book of Mormon*, Joseph Smith was taught the theme of Nephi as he translated the words of that ancient prophet. Additionally, Nephi had set a precedence of having multiple witnesses.

2 Nephi 11:3

3...wherefore, I will send their words forth unto my children to prove unto them that my words are true. Wherefore, by the words of three, God hath said, I will establish my word. Nevertheless, God sendeth more witnesses, and he proveth all his words.

And he had also set the precedence of his adding another, living witness—his brother Jacob (2 Nephi 6:1, 11:1), after the passing of his father who had that role (2 Nephi 1:1-12). Through this, Joseph Smith understood the need for another living witness, a witness in our dispensation, to be included with Nephi and testify of his theme. In essence, As he had been to Jacob, Nephi was Joseph Smith's "Samuel," calling him to prophesy among the prophets.

1 Samuel 10:1, 6-10

1 Then Samuel...said...

6 And the Spirit of the Lord will come upon thee, and thou shalt prophesy with them, and shalt be turned into another man.

7 And let it be, when these signs are come unto thee, that thou do as occasion serve thee; for God is with thee...

9 And it was so that when he had turned his back to go from Samuel, God gave him another heart: and all those signs came to pass that day.

10 And when they came thither to the hill, behold, a company of prophets met him; and the Spirit of God came upon him, and he prophesied among them.

Thus on the day, in that little room when Joseph Smith received and dictated those particular chapters to Oliver Cowdery into the manuscript of what we know as *The Book of Mormon*, Joseph Smith understood that he was called to be a prophet of God, to move forward confidently, for God would be with him.

The order in which these things were received by the prophet Joseph Smith is yet another testimony of the divinely inspired writing of, and process of bringing forth *The Book of Mormon*, and at the same time finishing the preparation and calling of the first prophet in this dispensation.

+ + + +

This brings us to one final point: Brigham Young taught that modern revelation was even more important than *The Book of Mormon*.

Ensign magazine June 1981: The Church of Jesus Christ of Latter-day Saints. "Fourteen Fundamentals of Following the Prophet" by President Ezra Taft Benson of the Quorum of the Twelve.

President Wilford Woodruff tells of an interesting incident that occurred in the days of the Prophet Joseph Smith:

"I will refer to a certain meeting I attended in the town of Kirtland in my early days. At that meeting some remarks were made that have been made here today, with regard to the living prophets and with regard to the written word of God. The same principle was presented, although not as extensively as it has been here, when a leading man in the Church got up and talked upon the subject, and said: 'You have got the word of God before you here in the Bible, Book of Mormon, and Doctrine and Covenants; you have the written word of God, and you who give revelations should give revelations according to those books, as what is written in those books is the word of God. We should confine ourselves to them.'

When he concluded, Brother Joseph turned to Brother Brigham Young and said, 'Brother Brigham I want you to go to the podium and tell us your views with regard to the living oracles and the written word of God.' Brother Brigham took the stand, and he took the Bible, and laid it down; he took the Book of Mormon, and laid it down; and he took the Book of Doctrine and Covenants, and laid it down before him, and he said: 'There is the written word of God to us, concerning the work of God from the beginning of the world, almost, to our day. And now,' said he, 'when compared with the living oracles those books are

285

nothing to me; those books do not convey the word of God direct to us now, as do the words of a Prophet or a man bearing the Holy Priesthood in our day and generation. I would rather have the living oracles than all the writing in the books.' That was the course he pursued. When he was through, Brother Joseph said to the congregation; 'Brother Brigham has told you the word of the Lord, and he has told you the truth.'" (Conference Report, October 1897, pp. 18–19, as quoted from an address at BYU in 1980, and then used in first presidency message in the Ensign magazine in 1981)

Brigham Young and Joseph Smith both testified of the importance of modern revelation over even written scripture. This means that as important as *The Book of Mormon* is to us, it is all the more important that it was used to train the first prophet of this dispensation, and thereby subsequent prophets, leaders and in fact it is an opportunity and clarion for all saints to receive revelation, which is the life-blood of true disciples of Jesus Christ.

CHAPTER 16

Banquet

There are still more feasts to be found in *The Book of Mormon.* And in light of the theme of Nephi, the gala may be as endless as revelation itself.

Some of the last words that Mormon included on the golden plates:

> **Words of Mormon 1:1,3-7**
>
> **1** And now I, Mormon, being about to deliver up the record which I have been making into the hands of my son Moroni, behold I have witnessed almost all the destruction of my people, the Nephites.
>
> **3** And now, I speak somewhat concerning that which I have written; for after I had made an abridgement from the plates of Nephi, down to the reign of this king Benjamin, of whom Amaleki spake, I searched among the records which had been delivered into my hands, and I found these plates, which contained this small account of the prophets, from Jacob down to the reign of this king Benjamin, and also many of the words of Nephi.
>
> **4** And the things which are upon these plates pleasing me, because of the prophecies of the coming of Christ; and my fathers knowing that many of them have been

fulfilled; yea, and I also know that as many things as have been prophesied concerning us down to this day have been fulfilled, and as many as go beyond this day must surely come to pass—

5 Wherefore, I chose these things, to finish my record upon them, which remainder of my record I shall take from the plates of Nephi; and I cannot write the hundredth part of the things of my people.

6 But behold, I shall take these plates, which contain these prophesyings and revelations, and put them with the remainder of my record, for they are choice unto me; and I know they will be choice unto my brethren.

7 And I do this for a *wise purpose*; for thus it whispereth me, according to the workings of the Spirit of the Lord which is in me. And now, I do not know all things; but the Lord knoweth all things which are to come; wherefore, he worketh in me to do according to his will.

Mormon included the small plates of Nephi for a wise purpose, and it is noteworthy that Mormon, in explaining the rationale of the inclusion at the end of his record, quoted the original writer in that author's explanation of why the record on the small plates was even created:

1 Nephi 9:1-6

1 And all these things did my father see, and hear, and speak, as he dwelt in a tent, in the valley of Lemuel, and also a great many more things, which cannot be written upon these plates.

2 And now, as I have spoken concerning these plates, behold they are not the plates upon which I make a full account of the history of my people; for the plates upon

which I make a full account of my people I have given the name of Nephi; wherefore, they are called the plates of Nephi, after mine own name; and these plates also are called the plates of Nephi.

3 Nevertheless, I have received a commandment of the Lord that I should make these plates, for the special purpose that there should be an account engraven of the ministry of my people.

4 Upon the other plates should be engraven an account of the reign of the kings, and the wars and contentions of my people; wherefore these plates are for the more part of the ministry; and the other plates are for the more part of the reign of the kings and the wars and contentions of my people.

5 Wherefore, the Lord hath commanded me to make these plates for a *wise purpose* in him, which purpose I know not.

6 But the Lord knoweth all things from the beginning; wherefore, he prepareth a way to accomplish all his works among the children of men; for behold, he hath all power unto the fulfilling of all his words. And thus it is. Amen.

They were created for a wise purpose, and they were included for a wise purpose. We should not imply from this that Nephi and Mormon did not know of good reasons that this record should be created and included in the golden plates. But we can infer that they may not have been privy to all of the reasons—which is an example of faithful discipleship to the reader—or that these reasons were not to be part of their record to us. We can demonstrate from the lives of each of these prophets that they were not required to move forward completely in the dark any more that the brother of Jared, who, through his faith and effort was able to light the barges for the long journey of his people.

> **Amos 3:7**
>
> 7 Surely the Lord GOD will do nothing, but he revealeth his secret unto his servants the prophets.

One of the reasons—that we know now—for the creation and inclusion of the small plates was to counter the problem with the lost manuscript. Given the difficulty in obtaining the gold, creating the plates, and scribing the record onto the plates, it might have been a bit frustrating for Mormon if he were made aware of this reason.

However, I do believe that Mormon understood that even though the small plates duplicated some of the timeline, the lessons to future leaders from these plates regarding the reception of revelation, made them a worthy appendix to his work. Evidence of this is found in Mormon's "intent" near the end of his writing.

> **Mormon 7:9**
>
> 9 For behold, this is written for the intent that ye may believe that; and if ye believe that ye will believe this also; and if ye believe this ye will know concerning your fathers, and also the marvelous works which were wrought by the power of God among them.

This was the something extra, the master's course for those who require a deeper dive into understanding the need of revelation, for those who understand that we are to follow Christ in all things:

2 Nephi 31:3,9-13, 16-17

3 For my soul delighteth in plainness; for after this manner doth the Lord God work among the children of men. For the Lord God giveth light unto the understanding; for he speaketh unto men according to their language, unto their understanding.

9 And again, it showeth unto the children of men the straitness of the path, and the narrowness of the gate, by which they should enter, he having set the example before them.

10 And he said unto the children of men: Follow thou me. Wherefore, my beloved brethren, can we follow Jesus save we shall be willing to keep the commandments of the Father?

11 And the Father said: Repent ye, repent ye, and be baptized in the name of my Beloved Son.

12 And also, the voice of the Son came unto me, saying: He that is baptized in my name, to him will the Father give the Holy Ghost, like unto me; wherefore, follow me, and do the things which ye have seen me do.

13 Wherefore, my beloved brethren, I know that if ye shall follow the Son, with full purpose of heart, acting no hypocrisy and no deception before God, but with real intent, repenting of your sins, witnessing unto the Father that ye are willing to take upon you the name of Christ, by baptism—yea, by following your Lord and your Savior down into the water, according to his word, behold, then shall ye receive the Holy Ghost; yea, then cometh the baptism of fire and of the Holy Ghost; and then can ye speak with the tongue of angels, and shout praises unto the Holy One of Israel.

16 And now, my beloved brethren, I know by this that unless a man shall endure to the end, in following the example of the Son of the living God, he cannot be saved.

17 Wherefore, do the things which I have told you I have seen that your Lord and your Redeemer should do;

2 Nephi 32:1-3

1 And now, behold, my beloved brethren, I suppose that ye ponder somewhat in your hearts concerning that which ye should do after ye have entered in by the way. But, behold, why do ye ponder these things in your hearts?

2 Do ye not remember that I said unto you that after ye had received the Holy Ghost ye could speak with the tongue of angels? And now, how could ye speak with the tongue of angels save it were by the Holy Ghost?

3 Angels speak by the power of the Holy Ghost; wherefore, they speak the words of Christ.

As mentioned, it is most likely that the small plates of Nephi were the last part of the golden plates that were translated by Joseph Smith. He translated the record by the power of God. and therefore we need suppose that he would have learned great things as he went through this process, even in just the first time through. It appears that at the time of translation, it was plain to Joseph Smith that the theme of Nephi was to teach leaders of the Lord's people, and indeed all of the Lord's people (if they would have it) how to receive revelation. Including also as a tool for same, the study and application of the somewhat abstract poetry we know as the Book of Isaiah.

As the initial student—in this dispensation—of Nephi's thematic process, Joseph Smith added his testimony to the work, just as Jacob had done. Nephi may have been focused principally on Jacob et al of the Nephites, but he was given to know that there was a secondary audience:

> **2 Nephi 26: 14-17**
>
> **14** But behold, I prophesy unto you concerning the last days; concerning the days when the Lord God shall bring these things forth unto the children of men.
>
> **15** After my seed and the seed of my brethren shall have dwindled in unbelief, and shall have been smitten by the Gentiles; yea, after the Lord God shall have camped against them round about, and shall have laid siege against them with a mount, and raised forts against them; and after they shall have been brought down low in the dust, even that they are not, yet the words of the righteous shall be written, and the prayers of the faithful shall be heard, and all those who have dwindled in unbelief shall not be forgotten.
>
> **16** For those who shall be destroyed shall speak unto them out of the ground, and their speech shall be low out of the dust, and their voice shall be as one that hath a familiar spirit; for the Lord God will give unto him power, that he may whisper concerning them, even as it were out of the ground; and their speech shall whisper out of the dust.
>
> **17** For thus saith the Lord God: They shall write the things which shall be done among them, and they shall be written and sealed up in a book...

He prophesied that in the last days, this record would be again made available.

The theme of Nephi clarified the role of Joseph Smith as a prophet, to the Prophet Joseph Smith. The body of work was instrumental in the restoration of the gospel of Jesus Christ in this final dispensation because mankind's understanding of the gospel is based upon revelation. Joseph Smith was to receive revelation; he was to speak with the tongue of angels, who speak the words of Christ.

> **2 Nephi 32:5-6**
>
> 5 For behold, again I say unto you that if ye will enter in by the way, and receive the Holy Ghost, it will show unto you all things what ye should do.
>
> 6 Behold, this is the doctrine of Christ, and there will be no more doctrine given until after he shall manifest himself unto you in the flesh. And when he shall manifest himself unto you in the flesh, the things which he shall say unto you shall ye observe to do.

Revelation through the Holy Ghost is the fountain of spiritual knowledge upon the earth. It is the whole doctrine, and why we can say that *The Book of Mormon* contains the fullness of the gospel. As Nephi said, there is nothing greater until Christ shall manifest himself unto us in person. And though such a personal manifestation is a great blessing indeed, God also blesses his children by withholding spiritual knowledge until we are prepared to be responsible for it.

There are additional ramifications in having this information, beyond just these three chapters:

Understanding this new and decidedly more modern voice in 2 Nephi 27-29 also helps us in exploring the other, shorter editorial found throughout the volume: Joseph Smith was learning these concepts while he translated and by the same power. This should be considered next time a verse containing "and thus we see" is read. Such as:

CHAPTER 17

Heroic Decisions

There are details of *The Book of Mormon* that somehow made the grade to be inspired by God to be written down by prophets of God, edited and etched onto golden plates by prophets of God, and translated by a prophet of God, that through common processes of study are excluded by the litmus of the topic in question. Some of these details are almost never returned to. It is natural that in subsequent examination of various passages our previous filters block these details and we, the students, become the cause of a certain blind spot in our learning. The use of macro-views is a useful way to enhance our ability to "feast upon the word of Christ." It is a way to explore *The Book of Mormon* allowing placement and alignment of even seemingly insignificant details one with another. Other methods of study are enhanced with an understanding of *The Book of Mormon* through the use of macro-views in that one might research a topic not only by key words but by ideas, by the thought processes of the inspired editors and (particularly as we have discussed in the case of Moroni) even changes over time in their thought processes.

The use of macro-views in our study of *The Book of Mormon* helps us to gather the seemingly insignificant flecks of information between the doctrine, and flecks of detail into the history of the lives of the individuals who wrote—and particularly who edited—the work. Through them we can see more of the unwritten: The day to day decisions that were made by the untimid in order to accomplish the command of the Lord: When the brother of Jared was commanded to build barges after the manner of the day, he moved forward and built them, and then went to the Lord to ask how to modify them for human cargo for long periods of time at sea. The Lord explained how to allow for the air, then specifically left the question of light up to the brother of Jared to solve. God left it to the brother of Jared to be creative and find a solution to the problem. It is not clear to me if there was more than one possible answer or not, but the solution that came into the mind of that faithful prophet was one that God would set his finger upon to support.

Likewise, we can read into the details that Mormon was called to abridge the records of the Nephites of which he had been given guardianship. This was the commandment of the Lord, and Mormon was left to his own devices to get it accomplished. He would need a lasting metal of which he would have known of only two: gold, or brass like that of the brass plates, that was specifically blessed to endure. He obviously would not have considered sacrificing any of the existing gold (or brass) record for their metal content for the new work. He needed gold. How does he accumulate 50-70 pounds of gold as a citizen of a nation retreating in disarray from a superior army? He made the heroic decision to recant his oath and return to lead the Nephite armies again. As he accumulated people to his army, he accumulated gold to the Lord's purpose of creating this record. He could have otherwise, and probably originally had planned to follow in the steps of Ether, who was called to stand back and record what happened. Leaving the area with all of the records in his charge would have been perhaps the safer way for himself, his family and for the records. But that is not the work that he was called to do.

He decided to become the general again. He decided to have the plates made. He abridged the Nephite record as commanded. He decided to train Moroni in the scribing of reformed Egyptian on gold plates. He provided Moroni with the Jaredite record and with custody of his record including blanks for the additional work. And in the end, He decided to provide Moroni safe passage so that his son could complete the work. He and Moroni decided that Moroni would go off on his own and complete the work of translation and the work of abridgement of the Jaredite record.

> **Doctrine & Covenants 58:26**
>
> 26 For behold, it is not meet that I should command in all things; for he that is compelled in all things, the same is a slothful and not a wise servant; wherefore he receiveth no reward.

God trains all of his children to be creative, perhaps preparing us for the hereafter. Just as God asks his prophets to create solutions in order to obey the commandments that he has given them, he asks each of us. Upon prayerful consideration, these solutions that come to our heart and mind are certainly inspired by God. When we ask for and receive the confirmation of the spirit, the implementation of these solutions becomes the will of God in the matter. Choosing to follow the will of God in doing our part to move his work forward is the expression of faith that multiplies our effort to make it possible to accomplish otherwise impossible things.

The ancient prophets were much like us: Pondering, praying and quietly making decisions every day as to how to take another step that will further the Lord's work here upon the earth. These are heroic decisions. From the editors of *The Book of Mormon*, only a few of these are etched into the plates and make it directly to our language and learning. They elected to keep a multitude of other decisions out of the holy writ. But a careful study and investigation of these scriptures helps us understand that their lives were like ours should be: Composed of good decisions, often heroic decisions.

END.

APPENDIX

Go to: nathanelambert.com for comprehensive tables of the writings of Isaiah as found in *The Book of Mormon*, that compare their usage to his writings as found in the Kings James version of The Bible and that indicate the various voices of the authors citing him.